FIRST PUBLISHED IN 2001 BY STRUIK PUBLISHERS

[A DIVISION OF NEW HOLLAND PUBLISHING (SOUTH AFRICA) (PTY) LTD]

CORNELIS STRUIK HOUSE

80 McKENZIE STREET

CAPE TOWN, SOUTH AFRICA

www.struik.co.za

NEW HOLLAND PUBLISHING IS A MEMBER OF THE JOHNNIC PUBLISHING GROUP

1 3 5 7 9 10 8 6 4 2

ISBN 1 86872 701 7

TEXT: GLYN DEMMER FOR NISSAN SA

MEDICAL INFORMATION: THE TRAVEL DOCTOR AFRICA AND DR ALBIE DE FREY

PROOFREADING: ANNELENE VAN DER MERWE

INDEXING: MARY LENNOX

DESIGN AND TYPESETTING: PLANET DESIGN

ART DIRECTION: PETER PRIMICH

REPRODUCTION: HIRT AND CARTER CAPE (PTY) LTD

PRINTING: CTP BOOK PRINTERS

THIS INITIATIVE IS SPONSORED BY NISSAN SOUTH AFRICA

AND DUNLOP TYRES (PTY) LTD

Contents

Foreword

Both Nissan South Africa and Dunlop Tyres share a belief in the future of off-roading. A harmonious balance between the utilisation of four-wheel drive vehicles and the environment is embodied in our credo: 'Tread with respect'.

The information and tips in this book have been gleaned through first-hand experience and passed down from fellow off-roaders. Information is presented in a concise manner for quick and easy reading.

Training, however, is a key ingredient and we strongly advocate that you attend an off-road driving course to gain some experience of driving in off-road conditions first-hand. This could save your life and prevent unnecessary damage to your vehicle.

We trust that this book will guide and assist you in the planning of your off-road trips throughout southern Africa and enhance your enjoyment.

We wish you many trouble-free hours exploring the beauty of our land, and remember – Tread with respect.

Tread With Respect

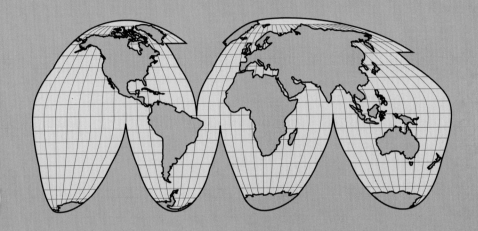

Tread With Respect

We live in an age of unprecedented freedom and 4x4 ownership is a wonderful adjunct to that freedom. But with this freedom comes responsibility and 4x4 owners have a duty to be sensitive to the environment in which they operate. Technology in the form of increasingly sophisticated off-road vehicles may have opened up new wilderness areas for exploration and private enjoyment, but it has also put an environmentally explosive device in our hands.

Environmentalists and the nature-loving public often charge that we are responsible for environmental damage, in particular to our coastal wilderness – and they have a point.

There has always been an element in the general 4x4 fraternity who are blind to the environment and who put self-gratification before the interests of their fellow citizens.

Responsible 4x4 owners, however, take a different view. They understand that we are custodians of our wilderness areas and that we must protect them for future generations. In a very real sense, this is a sacred trust.

But it is not only the 4x4 owner's sense of personal responsibility that must safeguard the environment – the State is monitoring the situation carefully as well. The tiny minority of 4x4 owners who have abused their privilege of access to our wilderness areas have brought the gaze of government, and the spectre of control, to the 4x4 market.

ENVIRONMENTAL AFFAIRS MONITORS THE SITUATION, ESPECIALLY IN TERMS OF BEACHES, AND REGULATION IS IMMINENT.

The number of vehicles on our beaches has increased dramatically and there has been consequent increased damage to coastal ecosystems and historical and palaeontological sites. As a result vehicles on our beaches generate an emotional response, notably from local communities wanting to maintain a pristine environment. There is always the danger that 4x4 owners could infringe the rights of other beach-users.

In order to protect the coastal environment, 4x4s have been restricted in coastal zones. It's currently being debated whether vehicles should be banned totally from the coastal zone or become subject to a permit system.

Although budgets have made policing difficult, the following areas were closed to recreational vehicles:

- Bathing areas with facilities for bathers.
- Beach areas adjacent to bathing areas which are used by the public for strolling.
- Ecologically sensitive areas, including dunes, estuarine salt marshes adjacent to estuaries, estuarine intertidal sand and mud flats, bird and turtle nesting areas, beaches with steep gradients or any other ecologically sensitive area.
- Protected areas specifically established to conserve the coastal environment, such as national parks, nature reserves and wilderness areas.
- Historical or palaeontological sites.

What this means for the off-roader owner is that in most cases a permit from the relevant authority is required to drive on the nation's beaches and even then we are required to drive only in demarcated areas along our coastline.

Legislation also requires that 4x4s only enter and exit demarcated areas via authorised access points.

Permits can be obtained from local authorities in the various coastal areas you wish to visit. They have the power to set fees, so these may vary from place to place.

You may well find that certain local authorities have not yet organised a permit system, but we recommend you still contact them for information.

So, what can we as 4x4 owners do to safeguard our precious coastal heritage? Here are a few guidelines:
- Drive only on beaches where vehicle access is permitted.
- Gain access to the beach via an authorised entry point.
- Ensure your vehicle does not have a petrol or oil leak – it will pollute the beach.
- Reduce tyre pressure before driving onto the beach or soft sand. Hard tyres cause excessive damage to the beach or soft sand.
- Where permitted, drive on the 'wet sand' section of the beach between the high- and low-tide marks, and remember narrow beaches may not be accessible at high

tide. However, consider local requirements in this regard – while turtle populations on the East Coast breed above the high-tide mark, on the West Coast crustaceans breed below this area. Consult nature conservation, if in doubt.

- Avoid bathing beaches.
- Avoid the following ecologically sensitive features: dunes, salt marshes, sand and mud flats, shell middens, drift material above the high-tide mark, pioneer plants on the backshore and bird and turtle nesting sites.
- Drive carefully – consider other people on the beach, your passengers, as well as other vehicles.
- Take all your litter home with you!
- Leave the beach via an authorised exit point.

DEFINITIONS

DUNES: these are vegetated ridges or sand areas next to the beach. Bad driving can erode dunes, destroy dune vegetation and is a threat to small mammals, birds and turtles.

THE BACKSHORE: this is the part of the beach above the high-tide mark. Drift material containing the seeds of beach plants accumulates here and wheels passing over drift lines destroy seeds and regenerating plants below the surface of the sand. High on the backshore, pioneer beach plants are destroyed by traffic. In some areas, animal life is also vulnerable.

THE INTERTIDAL BEACH: this lies between the low- and high-tide marks. As the intertidal beach is generally subject to powerful wave action and erosive forces, it is resilient and relatively resistant to vehicle impact. However, 4x4s can seriously erode steep beaches. Animal life on some intertidal beaches is vulnerable to traffic.

SALT MARSHES: vegetated, low-lying, flat areas that are periodically fed by salt water. One pass of a vehicle is sufficient to destroy salt-marsh vegetation that provides a habitat for crabs, shrimps, fish and birds.

SAND AND MUD FLATS: unvegetated, low-lying, flat areas that are periodically flooded by salt water. Like salt marshes, they are found along the shores of estuaries and lagoons. They are habitat to burrowing animals used for bait such as mud prawn. Pressure exerted by wheels can kill these delicate creatures and compact the sand into a hard, pavement-like surface.

SHELL MIDDENS: shell deposits where prehistoric people lived for extended periods. Middens are found along the entire South African coast, often on dunes. Some of the oldest middens in the world, dating back as much as 120 000 years, can be found along the Cape coast. Middens can provide valuable information about changes in climate, and animal and plant life; they also provide archaeological information about the lifestyle of earlier inhabitants. You know you have found a midden when both whole and broken shells as well as one or more of the following are found: bones and bone fragments, stone artifacts, ostrich eggshell fragments or beads, seashell beads or pendants, polished bone tools, pottery fragments, rounded stones with signs of burning, charcoal and/or ash. Off-road vehicles can destroy middens and with them the archaeological heritage of our country.

South Africa has a rich heritage. It is your responsibility as a 4x4 owner to preserve this heritage for the generations to come. That is why we promote safe, sensible driving.

TREAD WITH RESPECT

We owe it to fellow off-roaders and future generations to accept our role as responsible 4x4 owners:

- Act and drive responsibly and be courteous.
- Respect the rights of fellow off-roaders, local populace, and fauna and flora.
- Practise safe fire techniques.
- Remove your litter.
- Use cat latrines.
- Use biodegradable cleaners.
- Respect private land.
- Close gates.
- Avoid wheelspin and repair damage caused as a consequence of wheelspin – repack ruts, etc.
- Educate yourself – attend a 4x4 course.
- Use tree protectors when winching.

FUNDAMENTAL TERMS

DIFFERENTIAL TYPES

NORMAL OR CONVENTIONAL: an axle is divided into two half shafts, each driven independently by the differential side gears (bevel gears). This allows an inner wheel to turn more slowly than the outer wheel. The inside wheel thus turns more freely as power is transferred to the outer wheel which has less traction (otherwise the inner wheel would skid or scrub). Consequently, when off-road, a wheel without traction receives more power.

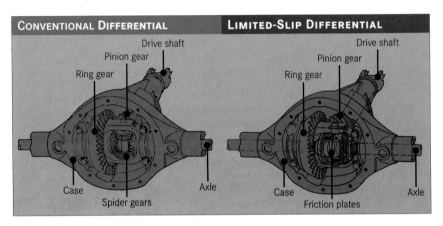

CONVENTIONAL DIFFERENTIAL — LIMITED-SLIP DIFFERENTIAL

Drive shaft, Pinion gear, Ring gear, Case, Axle, Spider gears, Friction plates

LIMITED-SLIP DIFFERENTIAL: a limited-slip differential limits this speed difference by mechanical intervention in a way that permits only a certain amount of slip to take place. The action is automatic, in most cases providing sufficient power to enable you to clear the obstacle.

AUTO LOCKERS: differentials that lock automatically when traction is required and unlock when variable rotation of wheels on a hard surface takes place. When in operation, power is equally split.

MANUAL LOCKING DIFFERENTIALS: these use a mechanical locking device operated by the driver; when locked, both axles turn at the same speed. May be pneumatic, hydraulic or electronic. If used when turning on a hard surface a characteristic scrubbing noise will be heard from the locked inner wheel. Pronounced use of this nature will result in accelerated wear.

CENTRE DIFFERENTIALS: a full-time 4WD vehicle needs a centre differential to prevent wind up between front and rear axles which is caused by the differential rotational speed on opposing wheels caused by cornering. In these vehicles the differential lock locks the front and rear drop shafts when going off-road.

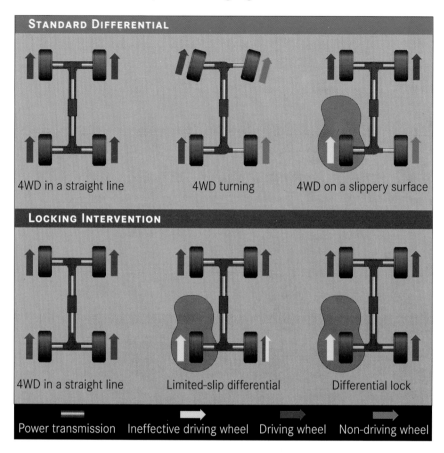

STANDARD DIFFERENTIAL

4WD in a straight line | 4WD turning | 4WD on a slippery surface

LOCKING INTERVENTION

4WD in a straight line | Limited-slip differential | Differential lock

Power transmission Ineffective driving wheel Driving wheel Non-driving wheel

TRANSFER CASE: an auxiliary gearbox offering high- and low-ratio gearing when in 4WD. In a part-time 4WD system the transfer case, when locked up, transfers power via the front propshaft to the front differential and thus through the side shafts to the front wheels. Front wheel hubs need to be locked for power to be transmitted to the front wheels. This may be an automatic or manual system.

TURBOCHARGERS AND INTERCOOLERS: diesel engines are well known for highly efficient operation. Performance can be enhanced through fitment of turbochargers and intercoolers. The turbocharger unit forces a greater volume of compressed air into the engine's combustion chamber, producing more power. This induction increases the temperature of the air. The air flow is directed from the turbocharger to the intercooler for cooling prior to entering the combustion chamber.

ENGAGING 4x4: generally you should engage 4x4 when going off tar and entering rough terrain. This gives better roadholding and reduces wear on your drive train.

4 HIGH (HIGH RANGE): all-wheel drive for mild off-road conditions allows higher-speed driving. High range can also be used on sandy conditions such as beaches where higher speeds result in a desired flotation effect.

4 LOW (LOW RANGE): all-wheel drive for low-speed, more extreme conditions requiring maximum power and traction. Low range can also be used in a higher gear on sandy terrain such as a beach.

Gear choice depends on engine type (petrol or diesel) and power output as well as individual ability and an understanding of vehicle capability. It is difficult to prescribe general gearing for various conditions.

GROUND CLEARANCE: the distance between the lowest point on the vehicle, normally the differentials, and the ground measured on a level surface.

WHEELBASE: the distance between the front wheel axle and the rear wheel axle, measured hub to hub.

ARTICULATION: the suspension's ability to follow varying terrain keeping all four wheels on the ground in a cross-axle situation.

TRAVEL: a shock absorber has two strokes – compression and rebound, both correcting suspension movement and keeping wheels in contact with the ground. Travel is the extent of the two strokes enabling the wheels to maintain contact with the ground.

Approach angle · Break-over angle · Departure angle

APPROACH/ATTACK ANGLE: simply put, this is the maximum angle at which you can enter into an obstacle without striking the obstacle. As it is determined by the location of the front wheels and the bumper valance combination, off-road ability can be enhanced by fitting a dedicated off-road bumper.

DEPARTURE OR EXIT ANGLE: the maximum angle at which you can exit an obstacle without fouling. Here towbars and drop plates come into play as they reduce the departure angle; when long-range fuel tanks are fitted, the spare wheel should be moved as this also influences the exit angle.

BREAK-OVER: the angle at which you can clear an obstacle without 'hanging up' between the axles, which is the point at which the underside of the vehicle would drag.

ROLL-OVER: the maximum angle at which a vehicle can traverse a side slope without rolling over. Obviously height, weight, load height and weight distribution will influence the vehicle's centre of gravity.

WADING DEPTH: normally specified by the manufacturer, this is the depth you can safely wade through water while keeping your air intake clear of the water – sucking water into an engine can be disastrous and cause costly damage.

Wading depth

Useful Equipment

Useful Equipment

THINGS TO TAKE ALONG

The perfect collection of equipment is usually created by experience. However, before you venture into the wilderness, you might want to consider putting together a few useful items in case of mishap. Hopefully you will never have use for them, but there is always that unexpected time when having emergency equipment can make the difference between adventure and disaster.

Some of the items mentioned below will be used in the course of any wilderness journey and, like your 4x4, will become good friends to you.

MAPS: these should always be folded and kept dry. It is wise to keep them in a sealed plastic folder.

COMPASS: this is a vital piece of equipment for any adventurer and would complement your GPS.

TORCH: the best is a compact, waterproof torch. Always check that the batteries are working. Take spare batteries along as well.

BINOCULARS: go for a small and robust make and keep them in a plastic bag, even if they are waterproof.

SUPER TOOL/KNIFE: this is an invaluable survival tool and should be mandatory equipment. Depending on your selection, this will give you reliable knife blades, a flat and Phillips screwdriver, scissors, can opener, wood saw, nail file, a chisel, reamer, a hook, and a corkscrew.

WATER: carry a good supply of water for each person and take water-purifying tablets or a water purifier.

STOVE: you have a choice between a small camper's stove that uses solid fuel, or a small gas stove with perhaps a spare gas canister. An army-style mess tin is ideal to cook meals and there are a number of sets of camping cutlery and crockery available on the market. And, of course, don't forget a mug.

SENSIBLE ADDITIONS: these would include 'Lip Ice' and sunblock, waterproof matches and a sewing kit.

In addition, it is important to take a sleeping bag, and many would argue that you should take a tent along as well.

SURVIVAL KIT

The survival kit is made up of a few key items that can make the difference between life and death and should be carried on your person at all times. Off-roaders usually pack a small tin and carry it in a pocket. It is a good idea, when venturing into very rough country, to keep additional vital equipment on your person as well. Following is a list of items to go into your survival kit:

Safety pins, thin wire, fishing line, hooks and sinkers, candle and matches, needles with large eyes and thick waterproof thread, a wire saw, antibiotic tablets, plasters, water-sterilising tablets, a magnifying glass, salt, a pencil, scalpel, a button compass, and a strong plastic bag. Old campaigners often use tobacco tins to store these items and they polish the lid so that it can be used as a reflector to attract attention.

FIRST AID KIT

No 4x4 owner should venture into the wilderness without a first aid kit of some sort. Your kit should contain items that will allow you to deal with most medical emergencies and help you to stabilise the patient until you can get proper medical help. Again you can buy ready made-up first aid kits, but it is often best to make up your own.

A good first aid kit would contain: plasters (limb, digit and spot), gauze dressing and bandage, crepe bandage, safety pins, painkillers, gauze padding, antiseptic wipes and antiseptic cream, triangular bandage, foot felt and corn plasters and a pair of high-quality scissors. You can add to this basic list as you please, the only real limitation being weight and the size of the kit – and your pocket, of course.

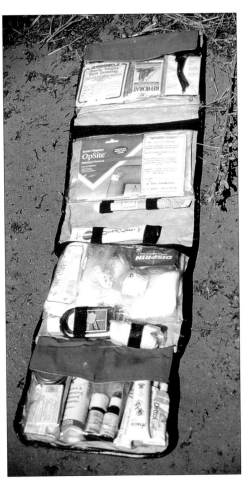

Medication should be kept in separate, easily accessible sections. Tubes and sachets are easier to pack than bottles and liquids.

If you are going to be travelling into very poorly developed and remote areas, consider adding sterile needles, syringes, intravenous cannulae and drip tubing for use by medical personnel en route. You should, however, not go overboard on these items – rather remember that **injections are seldom necessary** and much too keenly

23

administered in some settings. Avoid any injections or drips unless absolutely essential whilst travelling to avoid contracting hepatitis B or HIV.

Ask an experienced travel health consultant – preferably someone who often travels to remote areas – for advice on this topic.

Information on possible medical emergencies and the equipment you should take along to handle such emergencies is included on pages 29–31.

Following are just a few items which you should take along with you. Obviously your personal preference could make the list grow. The bottom line is – give this subject a lot of thought.

PACKING GUIDE

CAMPING PACKING LIST

This list covers most of the requirements for a long trip. It is unlikely that you would need to take along everything mentioned; the list is intended as a reminder only. Obviously you would need to choose your requirements based on the type of trip you are planning.

It is of major importance that you pack your gear so that you use space efficiently and the gear stays manageable. When travelling, the majority of your camping gear should be stored in metal trunks as follows:

- Tools and vehicle spares.
- Kitchen.
- Pantry.
- Photographic equipment.

- Separate foodstuffs, water and fuel.
- Pay attention to weight distribution.
- Ensure that your load is secure by using a combination of ropes and bungees. Fit additional tie-down points if necessary.
- If using an open vehicle, protect your load with a tarpaulin or tonneau cover.
- Wire baskets could hold reference books, maps, a travel file and flask.
- The insides of the lids of your trunks can also be converted to hold equipment.
- When packing for a trip, always practise with a dry run before leaving.

CHECK LIST

BEFORE TRIP
- ☐ Service vehicle
- ☐ Suspend phone service
- ☐ Place weapon in safekeeping
- ☐ Stop newspaper delivery
- ☐ Inform security company
- ☐ Set up answering machine
- ☐ Leave spare house keys with a neighbour or family

FURNITURE
- ☐ Tent – canvas/nylon
- ☐ Pegs, ropes & poles
- ☐ Awning sidewalls
- ☐ Ground sheet
- ☐ Fly sheet
- ☐ Lapa/windbreak
- ☐ Chairs/stools
- ☐ Tables
- ☐ Folding shelves
- ☐ Trunk stands

SLEEP
- ☐ Sleeping bags
- ☐ Mattresses
- ☐ Sheets
- ☐ Pillows and cases
- ☐ Head lamp
- ☐ Mosquito net
- ☐ Mosquito repellent
- ☐ Books/reading matter

BATH
- ☐ Toothbrush and toothpaste
- ☐ Soap and nailbrush
- ☐ Shampoo and hairbrush
- ☐ Shaving kit
- ☐ Towel and face cloth
- ☐ Toilet paper/caddy
- ☐ Tissues
- ☐ Body cream, sun lotion
- ☐ Bath plug, basin plug
- ☐ Nail file
- ☐ Roll-up wet pack

CLOTHING
- ☐ Rain/wind jacket
- ☐ Ponchos
- ☐ Sweatshirts
- ☐ Tracksuit
- ☐ Jerseys
- ☐ T-shirts
- ☐ Shorts
- ☐ Jeans
- ☐ Underwear
- ☐ Swim suits
- ☐ Socks
- ☐ Slops/sandals

- [ ] Shoes/boots
- [ ] Slippers
- [ ] Thermal tops
- [ ] Thermal bottoms
- [ ] Cap/hat/balaclava
- [ ] Gloves/scarves

COOKING AND LIGHT
- [ ] Stove fuel
- [ ] Stove gas
- [ ] Windshields
- [ ] Lamp fuel
- [ ] Lamp gas
- [ ] Torch/batteries/globes
- [ ] Spotlight
- [ ] Lighters & matches
- [ ] Plates, mugs, bowls
- [ ] Cutlery
- [ ] Bottle opener/can opener
- [ ] Corkscrew
- [ ] Bread board
- [ ] Kettle/pots/pan
- [ ] Skottel
- [ ] Braai grid/braai fork/tongs
- [ ] Potjie
- [ ] Pot-holder glove

TRUNKS
- [ ] Kitchen trunk
- [ ] Pantry trunk
- [ ] Tool trunk
- [ ] Spares/tool trunk
- [ ] Vegetable basket
- [ ] Strapping, bungees and tie-downs

FRIDGE AND WATER
- [ ] Fridge/freezer
- [ ] Water jug
- [ ] 'Coleman' cool boxes
- [ ] 'Isotherm' flask
- [ ] Hip flask

- [ ] Solar showers water purification system
- [ ] Water filter/tablets
- [ ] Water cans 10ℓ or 25ℓ
- [ ] Captap for water cans

FUEL
- [ ] Benzine/paraffin
- [ ] Meths/spirit jelly
- [ ] Gas cylinder
- [ ] Gas disposable cans
- [ ] Dual ext. arm
- [ ] Mantles
- [ ] Gauze for lamp glass
- [ ] Washers/seals/O-rings
- [ ] Stove spares
- [ ] Lamp spares
- [ ] Jerry cans for fuel requirements
- [ ] Funnel/spout
- [ ] Fuel-dispensing bottle

CLEANING (Bio-degradable please!)
- [ ] Sunlight cake soap
- [ ] Household cleaner
- [ ] Scourers and powder
- [ ] Dishcloths/wipes
- [ ] Carpet brush/pan
- [ ] Feather duster
- [ ] Braai grid brush
- [ ] Washing line
- [ ] Clothes pegs
- [ ] Windscreen cleaner

TOOLS AND VEHICLE SPARES
- [ ] Travel log
- [ ] Repair manual
- [ ] Super tool
- [ ] Screwdrivers
- [ ] Vice grips
- [ ] Pliers, short- and long-nose
- [ ] Side cutters
- [ ] Socket set

- ☐ Open-ended spanners
- ☐ Saw, blades and knife
- ☐ Shifting spanners
- ☐ Scissors, 'Tullen' cutters
- ☐ Wire brush or steel file
- ☐ Blowtorch and cartridge
- ☐ Fuel lines, vacuum lines
- ☐ Pre-filters, in-line
- ☐ Radiator hoses, top and bottom
- ☐ Clamps for hoses
- ☐ Fan belts and wipers
- ☐ Antifreeze
- ☐ Distilled water
- ☐ Jump cables
- ☐ Spare 12V battery
- ☐ Voltage meter
- ☐ Fuses
- ☐ Bulbs and car lights
- ☐ Electric cable lines
- ☐ Cable ties, small and large
- ☐ Nuts and bolts
- ☐ Spare wheel and 2nd spare
- ☐ Battery or hand tyre pump
- ☐ Tyre spanner and lever
- ☐ Tyre tubes and patch kit
- ☐ Tyre pressure gauge
- ☐ Triangles
- ☐ Hammer/mallet (1.8 kg)
- ☐ Spade for sand
- ☐ Axe and saw
- ☐ Bottle or high-lift jack
- ☐ Jerry cans
- ☐ Siphoning hose
- ☐ Fire extinguisher
- ☐ Duct tape
- ☐ Insulation tape
- ☐ Roll of wire
- ☐ Epoxy putty

- ☐ Contact and super glue
- ☐ 'Velcro' strip (pipe hose fix)
- ☐ Brake fluid and motor oil
- ☐ 'WD 40' and '3-in-I' oil
- ☐ Goggles (working under vehicle)
- ☐ Working gloves
- ☐ Handwash kit
- ☐ Spare car and house keys

OTHER GEAR

- ☐ Travel file
- ☐ Music
- ☐ Camera
- ☐ Binoculars
- ☐ Film – lots!
- ☐ Equipment-cleaning kit
- ☐ Maps and compass
- ☐ Book of the road
- ☐ Book on the area
- ☐ Reference books
- ☐ Sunglasses, nightglasses
- ☐ Spare glasses
- ☐ Notepaper and pens
- ☐ Contact phone numbers

BUREAUCRACY

- ☐ Passports
- ☐ Visas
- ☐ ID books
- ☐ International driver's licence
- ☐ Car registration papers
- ☐ Car insurance papers
- ☐ Triptyque (Zimbabwe)
- ☐ Third Party (non-SA)
- ☐ AA membership card
- ☐ Petrol card
- ☐ Credit card
- ☐ Cheque book
- ☐ Traveller's cheques

TRAVEL FILE CONTENTS

When planning a trip, always start a new file. Buy one with a clear plastic cover and in which you could insert clear plastic pockets in a clamp.

This file should be contained in a canvas holder complete with compass pocket, pen-holder and notepaper grip.

POCKET 1	**POCKET 5**
☐ Itinerary	Copies of
☐ Travel plan	☐ Traveller's cheque numbers
☐ Kilometre plan	☐ Petrol card number
☐ Fuel consumption plan	☐ Credit card number
☐ Places of interest	**POCKET 6**
POCKET 2	Empty pocket for
☐ Permits	☐ Collecting brochures
☐ Booking receipts	☐ Maps
POCKET 3	**POCKET 7**
☐ Car registration papers	☐ Main route map – there
☐ Car insurance papers	☐ Main route map – back!
☐ AA membership card	**POCKET 8**
☐ Triptyque (Carnet)	☐ Petrol receipts
☐ Third Party	☐ Accommodation receipts
☐ International driver's licence	☐ Other expenses
POCKET 4	**POCKET 9**
☐ Passports and Visas	☐ Packing list (so that you can make
☐ ID books	notes of what you have too much or
☐ Spare passport photographs	too little of) for your next trip

FOOD

As everyone's taste is different, we are not going to attempt a list. As with every aspect of your packing, careful planning is safest when putting together your menu. Calculate the number of breakfasts, lunches and dinners you will need to provide for, take the number of people into account, and try to plan ahead as to where or when you may be able to stock up. Try to divide your provisions into categories such as fridge items, meat, fruit, vegetables, tinned foods, drinks and juices, snacks and sweets, condiments such as salad dressings, sauces, jams, and dry foods such as bread, mealie meal etc., to make sure that you don't leave anything behind.

TIP: Have your meat and vegetables vacuum-packed, as this will help to keep them fresher for longer, something which is really useful if you are going to be away for a while.

TIP: Store bottles in plastic bags to prevent messy leakages.

One food item that can often be a problem is bread because it doesn't stay fresh for very long. Source a simple recipe for beer or pot bread and bake your own.

FIRST AID AND EMERGENCY EQUIPMENT

A first aid or emergency kit is essential. Take the most important items, as well as medication for anything you know you may be susceptible to.

We suggest that your first aid kit is packed in a soft-sided cooler bag with a zip closing, lined with a silver emergency blanket to keep heat out. Very strong see-through plastic pockets should be used as dividers and organisers. Label each pocket to avoid unnecessarily opening and soiling the contents when searching for an item in dusty conditions or rain.

List all items with their expiry dates and keep this list taped to the lid. Always keep your first aid kit stored in the coolest part of the vehicle.

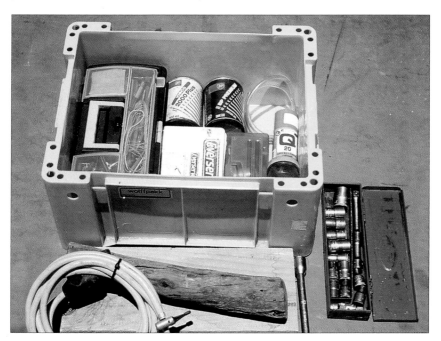

First Aid

MEDICAL

Prior to embarking on a long trip, you should pay a visit to your doctor or a travel health consultant (and dentist) to assess your general physical condition, discuss travel-related health hazards such as food- and water-borne disease, malaria prevention and prophylaxis, possible immunisation and the contents of your first aid kit.

The level of assistance you will be able to render if called upon depends on the training you have received. In a worst-case scenario, you should be able to cope with the areas covered. It would be worthwhile to undergo first aid training that includes updates if you are likely to venture into the wilderness on a regular basis. The following list is meant as a reminder/guideline only. Your doctor or pharmacist will be able to best advise you.

USEFUL EQUIPMENT
- ☐ Folding cup
- ☐ Disposable gloves
- ☐ Resuscitation valve
- ☐ CPR mouthpiece
- ☐ Long-nosed scissors
- ☐ Fine scissors
- ☐ Fine tweezers
- ☐ Flat-nose tweezers
- ☐ Silver blanket
- ☐ Blades
- ☐ Thermometer
- ☐ Clamps
- ☐ Safety pins
- ☐ Eye bath and patch
- ☐ Dropper
- ☐ Wide bandage and crepe bandage
- ☐ Gauze bandage and alcohol swabs
- ☐ Purified water (for wound cleaning)
- ☐ Plasters (variety)
- ☐ Bandage grips
- ☐ Cotton wool
- ☐ Swabs

MEDICATION
- ☐ Gastro-intestinal
- ☐ Loperamide (Imodium)
- ☐ Hyoscine (Buscopan)
- ☐ Metoclopramide (Maxalon)
- ☐ Aluminium/magnesium (Gelusil)

COUGHS
- ☐ Cough mixture
- ☐ Jamaican ginger
- ☐ 'Olbas'
- ☐ 'Medlemon' throat lozenges

PAIN AND SPRAIN MEDICATION
- ☐ Paracetamol (Panado)
- ☐ Diclofenac (Voltaren)
- ☐ Oil of cloves for toothache

TOPICALS
- ☐ Iodine preparation (Betadine)
- ☐ Steroid preparation (Dermovate

BURNS
- ☐ New skin
- ☐ Burn shields
- ☐ Paraffin gauze
- ☐ 'Combudoron' gel

EARS AND EYES	THINGS THAT COULD HAPPEN...
☐ Ear drops	Pain
☐ Eye drops	Diarrhoea
HOMEOPATHIC	Nausea/vomiting
☐ 'Rescue Remedy'	Dehydration
☐ 'Echinaforce'	Coughing
☐ 'Arnica' oil	Allergies
☐ 'Arnica' pearls	Itching
☐ Sinus drops	Blisters
☐ Wound powder 'Wecasin'	Rashes
KEEP IN FRIDGE	Stings/bites
☐ Purified water	Sinus
☐ Any medicines	Toothache
☐ Film (lasts longer in the fridge)	Period pain

PERSONAL EQUIPMENT PACKING LIST

Go through this list, live with it, then go through everything again. Nearly everything on this list requires discussion, explanation and comparison.

When backpacking, weight is of such paramount importance that great care must be taken to pack supplies of minimal weight, yet which will give you optimum performance. Foul-weather gear, in particular, must be selected with care, as often it can make the difference between life and death.

Packing and fitting of a backpack is a science in itself. Weight distribution and centre of gravity are major factors which can affect a hiker's comfort and health. An ill-fitting pack can cause spinal damage. Take great care that your pack is correctly fitted to suit your particular torso, height and shape.

BACKPACKING AND SLEEPING	COOKING AND LIGHTING
☐ Backpack	☐ Stove
☐ Closed cellmat	☐ Lamp or candle
☐ Ground sheet	☐ Fuel or gas cylinders
☐ Tent, poles, pegs	☐ Pots or billy cans
☐ Spare rope, cord	☐ Pot grip
☐ Emergency blanket	☐ Knife, fork and spoon
☐ Sleeping bag	☐ Mug and plate
☐ Pillow	☐ Water bottle and purifier

- ☐ Can opener or 'Swiss army knife'
- ☐ Matches and lighter
- ☐ Rubbish bags
- ☐ Biodegradable soap
- ☐ Scouring pad

TOILETRIES

- ☐ Toilet paper
- ☐ Tissues
- ☐ Toilet trowel
- ☐ Toothpaste and toothbrush
- ☐ Towel
- ☐ Sun block and body creams
- ☐ Lip balm
- ☐ Shaving kit
- ☐ Signalling mirror
- ☐ Hairbrush or comb
- ☐ Roll-up basin

FOOD (some ideas)

- ☐ Tea, coffee and sugar
- ☐ Milk powder
- ☐ Cereal
- ☐ Nuts and dried fruit mix
- ☐ Rye bread (it lasts longer)
- ☐ Butter or margarine
- ☐ Cheese
- ☐ Cold meats and smoked meats
- ☐ Packet soup
- ☐ Avocados (high in energy), carbo-loading keeps you warm
- ☐ Rice, pasta and 'Smash'
- ☐ Meat dish
- ☐ Vacuum-packed foods
- ☐ Nuts, sunflower seeds
- ☐ Energy bars
- ☐ Chocolate
- ☐ 'Granola' bars
- ☐ Fresh and dried fruit

CLOTHING

- ☐ Thermal wear
- ☐ Wool socks
- ☐ Underwear
- ☐ Very warm jacket (polar fleece is best)
- ☐ Track suit
- ☐ Woollen hat, balaclava or cap
- ☐ Gloves and scarf
- ☐ T-shirt
- ☐ Shorts
- ☐ Gaiters (to keep pants and socks dry in snow)
- ☐ Waterproof jacket or poncho
- ☐ Waterproof cover for pack
- ☐ Waterproof packing bag

MISCELLANEOUS

- ☐ Permits
- ☐ Camera
- ☐ Film
- ☐ Binoculars
- ☐ Walking stick (shoulder height)
- ☐ Maps
- ☐ Notebook and pencil
- ☐ Torch
- ☐ Survival blanket

WEATHER CONDITIONS

Weather conditions can obviously make a great deal of difference to your outdoor holiday. Try to determine the type of conditions expected before you leave, and plan accordingly. If you are unlucky enough to hit a storm, take great care to protect yourself from lightning. Do not expose yourself if at all possible during a storm. If you are caught outside, sit down or crouch on some form of insulation, even if it is only your sleeping bag. Do not seek shelter beneath isolated, tall trees, or other tall objects that attract lightning.

WATER PURIFICATION

As you are unlikely ever to be able to carry enough water with you to last your trip, one of the most important considerations when camping is the availability of water. However, there is often no way of knowing whether this water is safe to drink and in many African countries, including many parts of South Africa, it isn't.

Methods of water purification vary from tablets to sophisticated filtration units. When travelling, you should ascertain the condition of the water along the route and purchase suitable equipment.

MALARIA

With the rising occurrence of resistant malaria strains, taking adequate precautions to protect yourself against this potentially fatal disease is essential. 80–90% of reported cases of malaria occur in Africa; out of the approximately 5 million people per year who die from this disease, an estimated 1 million are children under the age of five.

Chloroquine has always been the anti-malarial medication of choice. However, it is no longer sufficient to take Chloroquine and consider yourself protected. It is important to identify first whether the malaria area you are entering is a Chloroquine-resistant area or a Chloroquine-sensitive area. Once you have determined this fact, your doctor or pharmacist will be able to advise you on the most suitable medication. Of course, prevention is the best medicine, and the most important factor in preventing malaria is preventing the bite in the first place.

ASSESSING MALARIA RISK

- Length of stay in malaria area.
- Time of year (i.e. dry season or wet season).
- Prevalence of malaria.
- Type of accommodation (outdoors or indoors).

- Your immunity: the elderly, babies, children under the age of five, pregnant women, or patients with low immunity are considered to be high risk.

PREVENTION

- Apply insect repellent to exposed skin and wear light-coloured clothing as insects are not attracted to light colours.
- Wear long sleeves and long trousers at night.
- Use mosquito nets, screens as well as insecticide coils or mats.
- Avoid going outside at dusk or dawn.
- Visit malaria areas during dry seasons or in years when rainfall is low.

ANTI-MALARIAL MEDICATION

NB: Side effects can be experienced when using anti-malarial medications. Dosage also varies, so before embarking on any course of medication, please consult your doctor or pharmacist for advice.

TIP: As Africa has become more accessible to travellers, numerous travel clinics have opened up – it is worthwhile consulting them before your trip.

TIP: In addition to malaria prophylactics take a test kit and malaria medication for self-medication. Consult your doctor!

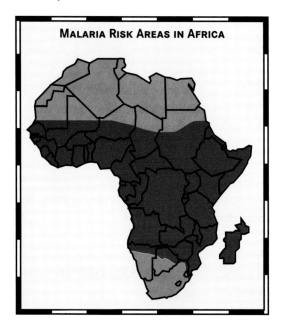

MALARIA RISK AREAS IN AFRICA

KNOTS

Nowadays we tend to rely on high-tech means of securing equipment such as ratchet straps, cable ties, tie-downs, and cargo nets. All too often we forget their forebear, the basic standby – a length of rope. Rope has been used for over 300 000 years, so it is a well-tried and -tested backup, and should be an indispensable part of every off-road kit.

Ropes are made of both natural fibres (hemp, cotton, manilla, or sisal) and synthetic materials (nylon, polyester, polyethylene, polypropylene, or high-tech materials such as Kevlar) and available in varying diametre cordages to suit almost any use. Rope construction may be divided into in four main types: laid, braided, plaited and sheath-and-core.

LAID: these ropes derive their geometry from twist and counter twist which is imparted during their manufacture. A typical three-strand rope of this type is known as a hawser. Hard laid ropes are longer wearing, but softer laid ropes make knot-tying easier.

BRAIDED: these ropes are common in synthetic materials and are more flexible and less prone to stretching than laid ropes. These ropes are also less prone to kinking.

PLAITED: these ropes usually contain eight or sixteen nylon ropes and are woven in pairs. They are usually used to moor ships.

SHEATH-AND-CORE: these ropes are commonly used in climbing and mountaineering. They are generally made of synthetic materials with a static or dyamic load rating. Static ropes are designed for greater wear resistance and the occasional fall of regular climbing, while dynamic ropes are used in safety applications and are designed to be extra elastic to cope with potentially disastrous falls in mountaineering. Seek professional advice in selecting the correct type of rope to take along on your trip.

In the off-road context, ropes can be used for many applications, from simply lashing a load, to rigging around a permanent campsite, to making snares to trap wild animals in an emergency survival situation.

We have included some of the more commonly used and most useful knots for off-roaders. As with all off-road techniques, the knots should be practised before departing on a trip as you never know when you might need them.

THUMB OR OVERHAND KNOT

This is the most basic stopper knot. It is useful to prevent thread or string from fraying or pulling out of a hole.

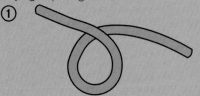 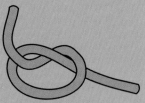

OVERHAND KNOT WITH A DRAWLOOP

This is an elaboration of the overhand knot. The addition of a drawloop makes it easy to undo the knot. It is especially useful on thin string which can be be difficult to undo.

FISHERMAN'S KNOT

The fisherman's knot is a very reliable and useful knot that can even be used at home or for fishing. It is based on the thumb knot and can be untied if made from rope, but will have to be cut if made with thread or string.

CLOVE HITCH

This is an easy knot to tie but can come adrift if subjected to jerking. It can also jam, so consider adding a drawloop.

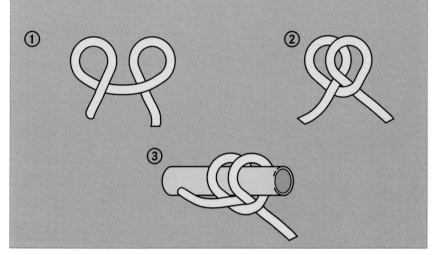

ROLLING HITCH

This is an elaboration on the clove hitch. It is intended to be used where lengthwise pulling is required.

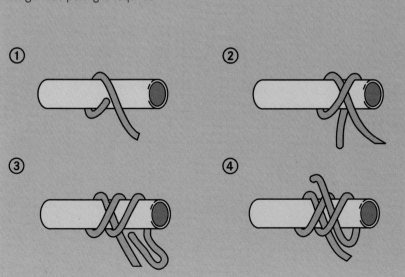

DOUBLE SHEET BEND

The double sheet bend knot is used to tie lines of dissimilar thickness or stiffness.

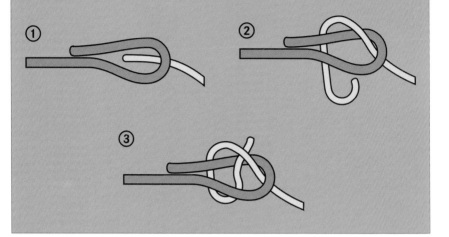

REEF KNOT

The reef knot is a more secure way of tying shoe laces. The reef knot can tend to bind. It is useful in tying bandages and small parcels.

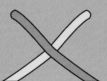

FIGURE-OF-EIGHT LOOP

The figure -of-eight loop tends to jam if wet. It is easy to tie and an alternative to the bowline. This knot is currently gaining favour with rock climbers.

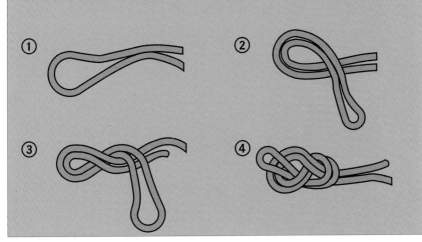

BOWLINE

The bowline is a very useful knot for tying all types of articles including parcels and can even be used in tree surgery. An advantage is that it does not slip, loosen or jam.

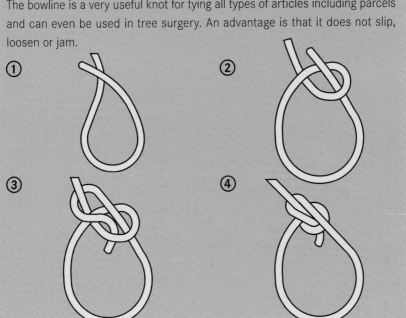

The trucker's hitch is used to lash down loads to your vehicle securely. This can be used in place of ratchet straps, cable ties, tie-downs or cargo nets if needed.

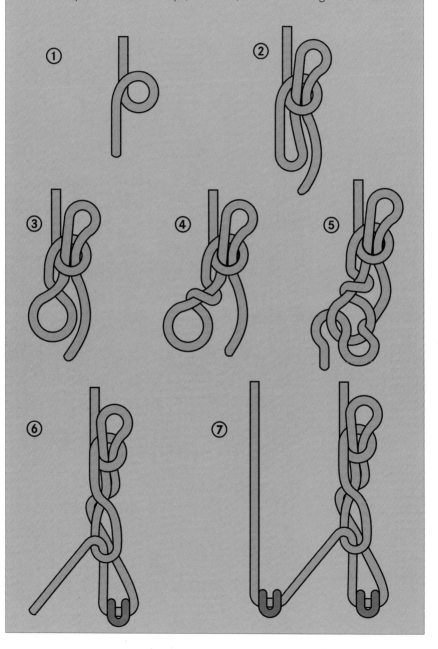

Marline hitching is ideal for lashing awkward objects or long loads, such as carpets, to lengths of tubing. Once the first binding loop has been tied, you need to maintain regular spacing and tension between the hitches to keep the pressure on the load constant.

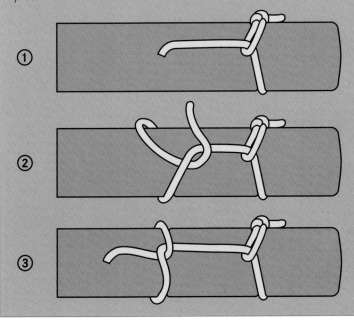

	COMPARISON OF NATURAL FIBRE AND SYNTHETIC FIBRE ROPE						
	Natural Fibre			Synthetic Fibre			
	Sisal	Cotton	Hemp	Polyethylene	Polypropylene	Polyester	Polyamide
Shock loading	•	•	•••	•	•••	••	••••
Handling	•	••••	•••	••	•••	••••	••••
Durability	•	••	••••	••	•••	••••	••••
Rot/mildew resistance	•	•	•	••••	••••	••••	••••
UV resistance	••••	••••	••••	••	•	••••	••
Acid resistance	•	•	•	••••	••••	••••	•••
Abrasion resistance	••	••	•••	••	••	••••	••••
Storage	dry	dry	dry	wet or dry	wet or dry	wet or dry	wet or dry
Buoyancy	sinks	sinks	sinks	floats (just)	floats	sinks	sinks
Melting point	n/a	n/a	n/a	±128°C	±150°C	±245°C	±250°C

Navigation

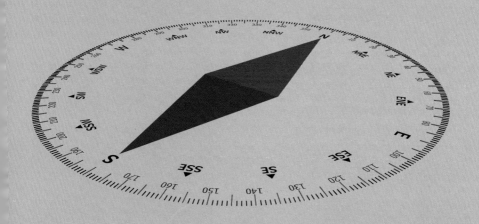

Navigation

COMPASS NAVIGATION

A compass uses a freely rotating magnetised needle or a card mounted inside a liquid-filled capsule; the needle of a compass (or the appropriate mark on the card) always points towards the magnetic north pole. The liquid in the capsule stabilises the needle and damps its rotation, giving the compass a quick and accurate response. The capsule – depending on the compass function – may be mounted into a flat baseplate or a spherical housing or some other shaped housing.

Various types exist but some features are of particular importance – specifically, the compass should be able to be used as a map compass, field compass and sighting compass.

A field compass is a plain compass that can be used to determine the direction in which you are facing or travelling; a map compass has various markings on the baseplate, and a rotating capsule. These features allow you to determine the bearing

(direction in degrees) of any feature on a map (north being zero, south being 180°
and so on); a sighting compass is a compass so designed as to be able to read the
bearing of any visible object relative to your (in other words the compass's) location.

Many compass models are available that fulfil all of the requirements listed above,
and with little practice you can use the compass to:
- Determine the bearing of a landscape feature.
- Determine the bearing of a map feature.
- Locate a map feature on the landscape by using the bearing of said feature.
- Locate a landscape feature on a map by using the bearing of said feature.
- Plot a course on a map and calculate bearing and distance of each waypoint on
  the course relative to each other.
- Navigate a course given several waypoints and their bearing/distance relative to
  each other.

WHAT YOU NEED TO KNOW WHEN USING TOPOGRAPHIC MAPS

A topographic map shows the lay of the land. Brown contour lines show the position
of hills, valleys and canyons. Green and white areas show the location of forests and
clearings. Blue depicts lakes, rivers and streams. Black is used to indicate features
such as backpacking trails and buildings. Other symbols show the position of ghost
towns, abandoned mines, ruins, marshes, swamps, waterfalls, springs, camp sites,
reefs, beaches, rapids, glaciers, tunnels, bridges, caves, and many other exciting
features. The map legend identifies these symbols. In fact, by looking at a topographic
map, you can pre-plan an entire trip right from your kitchen table!

SCALE

A map is a reduced representation of a section of terrain. Scale is the proportional distance between that on a map and the actual distance on the terrain. Scale is expressed as a ratio, i.e. 1:50 000. This means that 1cm on the map is equal to 50 000 centimetres on the actual terrain, or 0,5 kilometre.

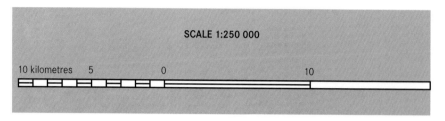

SCALE 1:250 000

10 kilometres   5   0   10

GRADIENT

Gradient is the rate of rise or fall on a stretch of terrain. Gradient is extremely important to an off-roader – always check the steepest gradient on your planned route. If your vehicle is capable of climbing that gradient, then you should have no problem with the rest of the route. Gradient is expressed as a ratio between the horizontal distance and the vertical rise/fall over that distance. Gradient is calculated on a map as follows:

Vertical Interval (VI) (height between contour lines)
Horizontal Equivalent (HE) (measure of the horizontal distance)

$$\text{i.e.} \quad \frac{\text{VI}}{\text{HE}} \quad \begin{matrix} = \\ = \end{matrix} \quad \frac{10 \text{ metres}}{500 \text{ metres}} \quad = \quad \frac{1}{50}$$

This means that the slope is a gentle one, rising one metre for every 50 metres you travel.

CONTOUR LINES

A contour line is a continuous line on a map which joins points of equal height above sea level. As such, they show the general shape of terrain and indicate features such as hills, mountains, cliffs, slopes, valleys, etc. Close contour lines indicate a steep gradient; when the lines are further apart, they indicate a gentle gradient. Interval spacing varies and your map should indicate the intervals. This should be checked to enable safe planning (a general interval between contour lines is 10 metres).

Many outdoor dealers who sell compasses also sell topographic maps for the areas near them. The best source of topographic maps is the Government Printer.

Map Key

International Boundary	
Provincial Boundary	
Railway Station or Siding	
Other Railway, Tunnel	
Power Line	
National Freeway	
National Route	
Arterial Route	
Main Road	
Secondary Road	
Other Road	
Track and Hiking Trail	
Lighthouse	
Mine	
Telecommunications Tower	
Monument	
Battlefield	
Post Office	.P
Police Station	.PS
Store	.W
School	.S
Place of Worship	.K
Hotel	.H
Trigonometrical Station	
Perennial River	
Non-perennial River	
Pipeline and Canal	
Marsh and Vlei	
Waterpoint	
Perennial Pan	
Non-perennial Pan	
Dry Pan	
Protected Areas	
Woodland	
Built-up Area	

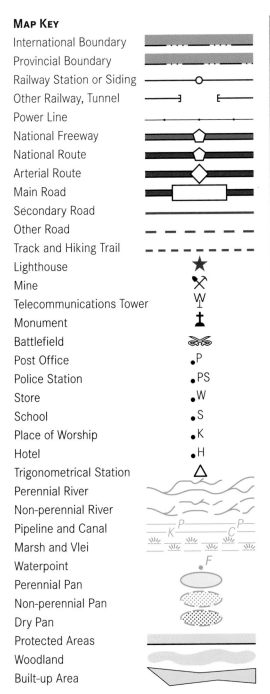

47

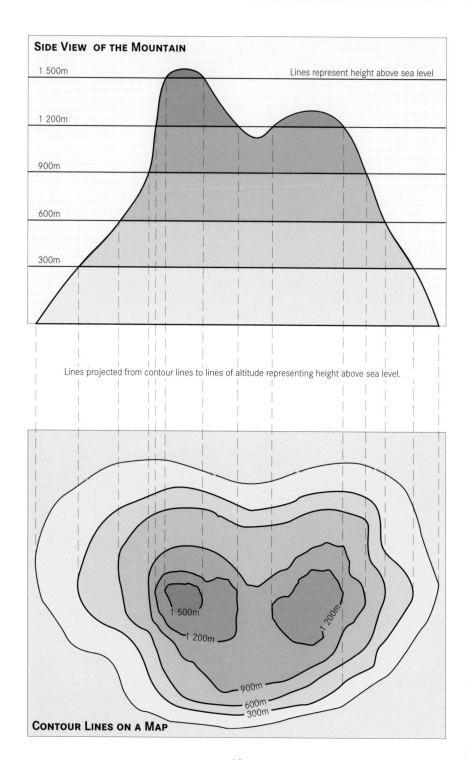

SIDE VIEW OF THE MOUNTAIN

1 500m — Lines represent height above sea level

1 200m

900m

600m

300m

Lines projected from contour lines to lines of altitude representing height above sea level.

1 500m
1 200m
1 200m
900m
600m
300m

CONTOUR LINES ON A MAP

WHERE'S THE NORTH POLE?

The spot map-makers indicate as the North Pole (Geographic, or True North – TN) is actually situated about 800 kilometres north of the pole (Magnetic North – MN) that attracts compass needles.

As a result there can be a difference between the direction your compass arrow shows as north, and the north indicated on your map. This difference is called magnetic declination. The amount of declination varies from place to place, so when using a compass with a map, the compass reading must be slightly adjusted.

- A compass always indicates magnetic north, which is approximately 19°–20° west of true north in southern Africa.
- With most compasses, you must add or subtract the amount of magnetic declination to get an accurate heading (for map bearings, subtract from the compass heading; add to a map bearing to obtain a compass heading).
- With many compasses you can preset the compass dial for magnetic declination and get an accurate reading automatically.

GPS (GLOBAL POSITIONING SYSTEM) NAVIGATION

GPS is a satellite-based navigation system, developed and controlled by the US Department of Defence. It provides accurate measurements of positions and altitude relative to sea level 24 hours a day, anywhere in the world. The system uses 24 satellites, each with an orbit time of 12 hours circling the earth at a height

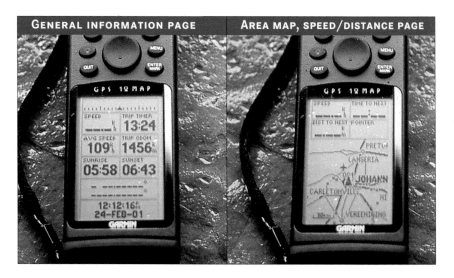

of 20 000 km. By using the signals from any four or more of them simultaneously, absolute positions and altitude can be calculated. GPS receivers are used by geologists, marine navigators and aircraft navigation systems, but they are also available in small hand-held models – around the size of a large calculator – for recreational or private use. They can be used in cars, boats or helicopters or carried by hand. GPS receivers typically store more than 100 waypoints (points along a course) to which you can get accurate readings on distance, bearing, estimated time of arrival, course correction and more. As an example of GPS use, you could store the location of your camp in the GPS memory (a waypoint) when setting out in the morning, switch off the GPS and place it in your vehicle or backpack. Later when you want to return to your camp, you can turn on the GPS and follow the reading it gives you to within 100 metres of your stored location.

TYPICAL GPS FEATURES ('PAGES')

- Waypoints – this is what the GPS is all about, making waypoints and going to waypoints. Today it is worth the additional expense to purchase a GPS with map features that correlate to the actual terrain you will be travelling through.
- Satellite status – signal strength, location, accuracy and battery strength.
- Position – location, heading, speed, average speed, sunrise/sunset. This page shows you your position and is used when you have not selected a specific destination.
- Map page (if applicable) presents position, features such as roads, rivers and towns. Here you are shown your actual movement which appears as a dotted line while you travel.
- Compass page – steering guidance.

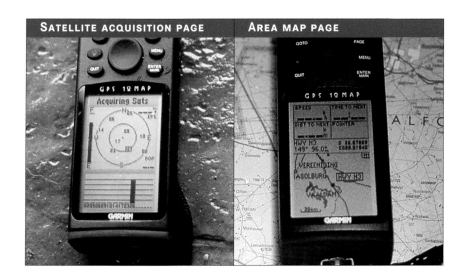

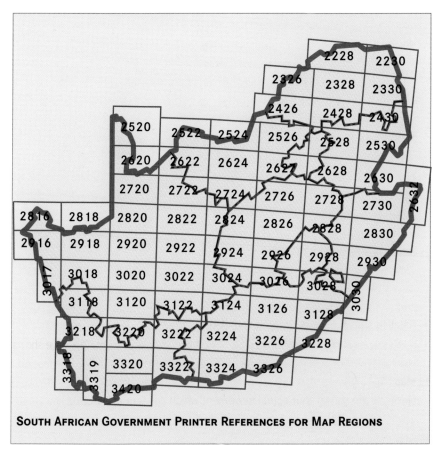

South African Government Printer References for Map Regions

51

Camping

Camping

CHOOSING YOUR CAMPSITE

Certain basics are applicable to the choice of a campsite whether you are out in the bush, in a national park or simply in a general resort.

In keeping with the philosophy of not breaking new ground and not deviating from a driven track when in your vehicle, you should also try to camp in an existing spot. Always arrive before sunset – there is no value in selecting your site at night.

Generally you should look for:
- A well-drained flat spot.
- Water.
- Wood (a campfire is always pleasant even if not used for cooking).
- Safe surroundings.
- Access to ablutions.
- Privacy (not too close to adjacent campers).
- Rubbish disposal – only applicable in national parks, caravan parks, etc. In the wilderness you should take all litter with you – leave no evidence of your visit.

Do not camp in dry river beds. Many a campsite has been devastated by flash floods; even vehicles have been washed away.

Be careful when camping directly under trees as these can be inhabited by small animals, insects and snakes with the consequences ranging from droppings on tables and tents to poisonous bites. Beware of poisonous snakes, baboons, monkeys and small predators – do not leave meat or cooler boxes out at night.

It is also prudent to avoid areas where branches or rocks can fall onto tents, people or vehicles.

Rivers, lakes and marshes are generally mosquito-infested. Besides being irritating, they can also carry malaria in many parts of Africa.

EXPOSING YOUR CAMPSITE
Hot air rises, therefore ridges and plateau areas are generally warmer than dips and valleys. This rule applies both in winter and in summer when dips and valleys will be cooler.

You should note the direction of the sun and camp in an area where the sun arrives early.

Choose a location that will provide protection from prevailing winds. Vehicles can also be sited to double as windbreaks.

ESTABLISHING YOUR CAMP
No matter how long you will be staying in an area certain basics exist.

Pitch your tent with the rear wall or the area opposite the door facing into the wind. Preferably face your door towards the campfire, but your tent should be at least 8–10 metres from the fire (to avoid flames, sparks, embers and ash).

If you must wash dishes in a river, wash midstream, between your drinking water area and clothes wash area. Scrape food away with sand or a cloth before rinsing, as food remnants will pollute the water and attract animals. Do not use detergents.

Collect drinking water upstream of the campsite, as well as animal water holes.

Smoke from a fire will keep insects away, but flames should be far enough away to avoid setting your tent alight (8–10 metres).

Position your tent entrance away from the direction of the wind.

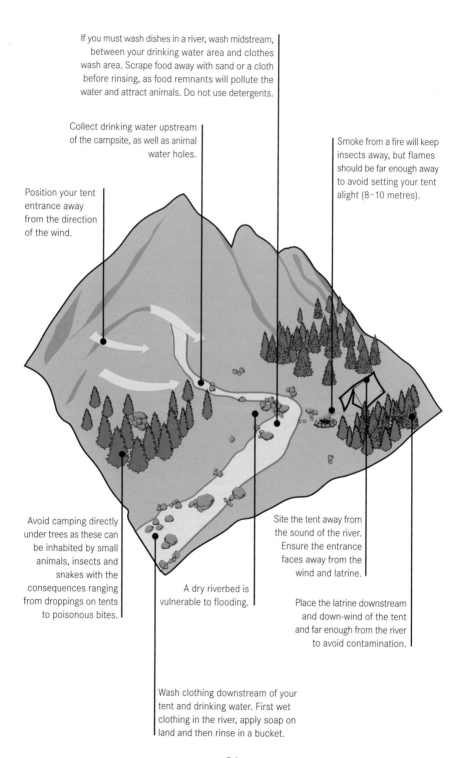

Avoid camping directly under trees as these can be inhabited by small animals, insects and snakes with the consequences ranging from droppings on tents to poisonous bites.

A dry riverbed is vulnerable to flooding.

Site the tent away from the sound of the river. Ensure the entrance faces away from the wind and latrine.

Place the latrine downstream and down-wind of the tent and far enough from the river to avoid contamination.

Wash clothing downstream of your tent and drinking water. First wet clothing in the river, apply soap on land and then rinse in a bucket.

Build a proper fireplace and use a stone retaining wall if possible, or, alternatively, site your fire in a trench.

Locate your toilet site. As a rule of thumb (depending on the number of campers, etc.) it should be 75–100 metres downwind from the campsite. Do not site a toilet in an exposed area or near a river, water hole or in soft soil.

Be aware of your water source if in a wilderness area. This will also assist in locating your ablution area for brushing teeth, shaving and showering. On no account should any ablution waste be allowed to drain into rivers. Always use biodegradable, environmentally friendly products (soaps, shampoos, toilet paper, etc.). Under no circumstances should you camp in close proximity or alongside a water hole or drinking point for animals. This has been known to deprive animals of their only water and in the case of larger animals can also endanger campers.

LAYING OUT YOUR CAMP

Taking the previously mentioned factors into consideration will help you to lay out your camp. The amount of equipment you unpack from your vehicle will be determined by the duration of your stay and the availability of ablutions, water, etc.

1. Pitch your tent and organise interior comforts.
- Lighting.
- Stretchers/sleeping bags/air mattresses, etc.
- Toiletries.
- Clothing.

2. Locate and organise your fireplace (stock up with firewood; protect your firewood from rain if you rely on the fire for cooking). Clear the area (2-metre radius) of inflammable material and use prevailing winds to dissipate smoke. Protect your flame naturally in windy or rainy conditions.

If you are not carrying firewood you will need to collect kindling to start the fire and wood for the main body of the fire. This task should be allocated on arrival at a site as there is nothing worse than blundering around in the dark looking for wood. Take care not to collect green wood as the resultant smoke is extremely unpleasant. Do not break trees and destroy the vegetation. In Africa there is generally enough suitable wood lying around for a fire. Be careful when lifting logs as insects and snakes reside under them. A tip would be to roll the log over prior to lifting it (use your boots) and do not be embarrassed to wear protective gloves when lifting and carrying wood – your hands need the protection from splinters, thorns and insects. Do not carry large logs too close to your body as ants, other insects, etc. could decide to leave their host.

BASIC FIRE SAFETY

- Clear area in a 2-metre radius.
- Build fire protection. Don't make a fire on the dripline of a tree – at this point roots are close to the surface.
- Relate the size of the fire to your requirements.
- Stock up on fuel (preferably carry charcoal as your primary fuel source).
- Shelter fuel from rain.
- Keep adequate stocks of matches (dry), firelighters or starters and do not be ashamed to keep a backup disposable lighter.
- Don't use wet fuel.
- Don't light your fire on grass, under a tree or next to a stump or log.
- Be aware of the type of wood you burn, as a wood such as tamboti produces an extremely noxious smoke which can be detrimental to your health (the same applies to any form of milkwood).

- Do not leave equipment of any nature close to the fire – especially gas bottles or liquid fuel.
- Protect your hands when removing kettles, pots, etc. Most cooking equipment has metal handles which get warm. Modern pots are designed to disperse heat, but do take care.
- An unusual way of protecting matches for emergency use is to set a small box and striker into melted candle wax; alternatively use a small, waterproof container.
- Don't leave camp until you have put out the fire and disposed of the waste.
- Establish your cooking and eating areas (tables/chairs) as well as your washing up area. Your waste disposal area should be sited away from the cooking area. It is important to note that waste and supplies attract animals who have a keen sense of smell. Bin bags can be shredded and the contents scattered over a large area. Coolers can be destroyed by hyenas or elephants attempting to get to contents such as meat, fruit, etc. These should be kept in steel receptacles and secured inside trailers at night.

- Minimise packaging by the way you plan your trip. Foodstuffs and dry ingredients should be transferred to containers which form part of your kit – prior to departure.
- Do your washing up immediately after a meal to avoid attracting flies, ants and insects. This will also avoid the spread of bacteria. Fat or grease can cause unpleasant stomach upsets.
- Do not wash up in or near rivers. Preferably use a portable fold-up basin. Store your cloth and scourer in a plastic container with an airtight lid.

Litter Tips

- To be environmentally friendly, carry out all litter which cannot be burnt.
- Pack plastic and other waste into small bags and put them into a large bin bag for disposal elsewhere, either at home or at a suitable point en route. It is no longer acceptable to bury scraps or waste.
- Paper and cardboard can be burnt on a fire (small quantities).
- Do not burn plastic.

Ablutions

Bathing

Although you are escaping from civilisation, you cannot ignore basic hygiene. If no formal ablutions exist, you can either use one of the many portable showers available on the market (ranging from solar-powered to similar units that can be filled with hot water) to a simple sponge-and-rinse technique. Teeth must also be cleaned on a regular basis. Do not let waste water drain into rivers or streams and don't forget to use biodegradable products. Bodily functions are a fact of life and cannot be ignored. Take a bathroom pack to your bathing area. This pack should include a wet cell, change of underwear and slippers or sandals. Always include a meathook to enable you to hang the bag up. Take a rubber chamois to use as a bath-mat and a fold- up basin to stand in if floors are suspect.

Toilets

- Chemical toilets are available but can be somewhat bulky – waste will have to be disposed of at the end of the trip.
- A good technique is to site a cat latrine – dig a hole and set a conventional toilet seat mounted on a stand over the hole. Once the campsite is vacated the hole can be filled in. It would also be worthwhile to lay stones across the hole prior to filling it with sand. Campers should learn to throw in a layer of sand after each use. A useful 'occupied' sign is to position a spade and roll of toilet paper halfway

between the campsite and the facility; if the spade is not in position the toilet is 'occupied'. On no account should any chemicals be thrown into the hole.

Toilet paper should be burnt rather than buried.

Campsite Equipment
Equipment for the comfort of campers has been adequately covered in the packing section (see page 24); however, some of the options available will be discussed in more detail below. Obviously, the type and choice of equipment will be determined by budget, frequency of use, climatic conditions, etc.

Tents
Nowadays tents are lightweight, easy to erect and, depending on the frame, quite sturdy. Better designs include integrated groundsheets, mosquito nets, bow frames and zip-up doors. Avoid any tent that requires plans and time to erect.

Discuss your needs with a reputable camping supplier – do not compromise on quality and look for:
• A tent that is easy to pitch.
• Suitable size and weight.

- Breathable fabric.
- Fully waterproof.
- Sealed floors.
- Mosquito nets.
- High-quality zips.
- Windows.
- Light, reflective colours.

BEDDING

You will have to give your camping shop a good deal of input before they will be able to supply you with a sleeping bag.

Your bag, be it of a natural fabric or synthetic, must suit your requirements. Apart from your vehicle, this may be your most important consideration. Beware of products which are not locally manufactured and which have not been developed for local conditions (CSIR or SABS ratings are important).

Properties to evaluate include:
- Hygiene and possible allergy to filling.
- Warmth-to-weight ratio.
- Cleaning.
- Absorbency and porosity.

COOKING EQUIPMENT

The most effective heat source in terms of heat generation is the benzine/paraffin stove which can burn either fuel with minimal changes. These stoves are small, safe and economical particularly when using paraffin (which is available throughout Africa). In fact, a single tank can burn for between three and eleven hours depending on the heat setting. Investigate pot sets which are light, space saving and heat efficient.

Your final requirements other than those detailed in the packing section (see page 24) will be:

- Tables and chairs.
- Fridges.
- Cooler boxes.
- Utensils.
- Water and fuel containers.
- Pots, pans, etc.
- Lights, torches, etc.
- Mattresses or mats.

The above are primarily determined by budget and space; a wide variety of good-quality items are available. Give a lot of thought to these items before buying. Consider your destination when deciding on your cooking equipment as a lot depends on the availability of fuel. Dry rations are also important and you should check all regulations pertaining to the transporting of fresh meat, especially in those areas where Foot and Mouth control points exist. Always remember to separate your utensils, rations and cooking equipment into rigid containers that can be closed.

Negotiating Your Path

Negotiating Your Path

Seasoned off-roaders know that the slower you enter into difficult obstacles, the quicker the recovery process will be should you get stuck, and it will also be less costly!

It all boils down to the basics of choosing your 'line' (or route) through an obstacle. Your ability to read terrain and define the path of least resistance, combined with your driving skills and knowledge of your vehicle's abilities, will see you safely home. **'The line':** you should attempt at all times to keep all your wheels on the ground, thereby gaining maximum traction. Do not be afraid to stop and rebuild a section before negotiating it, and always assess the obstacle before continuing – this means stopping and **walking your route** (if there is no danger from wild animals).

TIP: Avoid a dangerous obstacle if you are not totally confident that your whole group will safely pass through. The longer route will more than likely see you all home without any damage to vehicles.

TIP: Secure all loose equipment in rough terrain.

Your 4x4 certainly has the torque to take you almost anywhere and get you over most terrain, but driver and machine have to work in unison. At the end of the day it is the driver who makes the difference, and this section contains a few hints for off-roaders to help them handle the rough stuff when they come to it.

As in all things in life, practice makes perfect and it may well be in your interest to practise a few difficult situations before you put yourself and your new 4x4 at risk in some remote part of the wilderness. The benefits of an off-road driving course cannot be dismissed!

TIP: Get to know your vehicle's capabilities, angles, etc.

A lot of off-road driving is a matter of common sense. If you think the terrain you are approaching could not be covered by an ordinary vehicle, engage four-wheel drive before you take it on. It is no slight on your ability to stop before you take on the rough terrain and take a long hard look at the land. A few minutes could save you a few days in the workshop.

Remember, too, that in rough terrain, engaging four-wheel drive reduces wear on your drive train. If you have free-wheel hubs, lock them as you enter rough terrain as you can engage your front wheels (via your transfer lever, following the procedure applicable to your vehicle) from inside the cab when necessary. Don't forget to wear your seatbelt. Also remember to let the steering wheel slip through your hands as you coax the vehicle on course, working in tandem as you guide your vehicle. If you try to fight it, you might injure a finger or thumb should the steering wheel kick back.

DRIVING HINTS

We've compiled a few hints for off-road obstacle-crossing that may come in handy.

DRIVING IN MUD: Engage four-wheel drive and lock differential(s). Try, if possible, to stay in the middle of the track. Select the right gear before you take on the mud. Remember the lower the gear, the greater the chance of wheelspin, while a higher gear may necessitate a gear change and loss of forward movement. Never do anything sudden in mud. If the wheels start spinning, decelerate delicately. Try to keep up a steady speed and the steering wheel straight ahead. If the wheels continue to spin as you decelerate, you may well get stuck, but it is better to stop than to dig yourself in even deeper by accelerating madly. Swinging the steering wheel back and forth while the vehicle is moving in mud may help you get traction. If you have broad tyres, the best way to attack mud is with momentum. The spinning wheels tend to throw the mud aside and the vehicle's forward momentum is maintained. Be careful of hidden obstacles and try not to build a wall of mud in front of your vehicle.

DRIVING IN WATER: Always wade the water hazard first, checking for ruts, rocks and potholes underwater. The depth of water a vehicle can comfortably handle is usually specified. If, however, you need to wade deeper, don't stall if the water level is higher than the exhaust as this will make restarting difficult. And remember, engine revs should be kept low.

TIP: Use a long stick to probe ahead of you as you wade.

The secret is to engage low range and enter the water slowly. Avoid splashing into the water, which could drown your electrical system. Drive so that you create a clear bow wave which minimises water entering the engine compartment. Apply a silicone water repellent to protect your vehicle's electrics.

In the case of running water, test the strength of the river before entering. If you can't walk against the flow, don't try crossing. If the conditions are such that you decide to cross, drive diagonally across the flow.

TIP: Try to aim for a point across the river and concentrate on that point!

Once you've made it to dry land, give the vehicle a checkout. You may be exhilarated by your safe crossing, but don't forget the vehicle that got you there.

The best test in wading is, of course, common sense. If it looks treacherous or dangerous, it probably is, so why take a chance? If you have no option, proceed with care and try to stick to the manufacturer's recommendations.

Should you run into trouble, switch your engine off – before you suck water into your engine's air intake.

TIP: Fit a wading sheet over your grille to keep out excess water.

TIP: Don't wear seatbelts in water and keep windows open in deep water. If you get into trouble, you can escape via the open window. In shallow, long crossings, close

your windows and run your fan or airconditioner to build up a positive air pressure and prevent water seeping into the driver's cab.

Tip: If in doubt, reverse in. This pushes water away and lowers the water in front of your vehicle – you can drive out easily and access your winch if needed.

Tip: Be aware that oil expands in transmission components when they are hot – contraction from sudden cooling when driving in water causes a vacuum which may suck water in through your transmission's breather pipes. For short water crossings you may plug these breathers, however, and prior to a trip you can re-route these breather pipes to a position higher up in the engine bay.

Driving in Sand and on Beaches: Deflate your tyres (45% of normal pressure is about the limit) if you don't have broad tyres designed for driving through sand.

Again engage four-wheel drive before you enter the sand, making sure your free-wheel hubs are locked.

Try high-range first gear before you hit the sand or, if it is very thick, try low-range third. Don't change gear in thick sand and remember the higher the gear, the greater the chance of having to make a gear change; the lower the gear the greater the chance of wheelspin.

Try to stick to the tracks of other vehicles, and when you decide to stop, don't apply brakes. Look for a firm spot and simply let the vehicle stop under its own momentum. When you start up again, or if you get stuck in sand, try reversing a short distance before moving forward again.

Many of the tips relating to driving in sand apply to beach driving as well. You should always carry a silicone water repellent, a tyre pressure gauge and pump when driving on the beach.

Once again use your common sense. Logically the best time to drive on the beach is when the tide is receding. This will give you additional time to dig yourself out before the tide turns and you get caught and have to call in a recovery team.

Drive close to the water because that is where the sand is firmest, but beware of shiny patches, which indicate sand deeply saturated with water.

Avoid beach areas covered with pebbles or shells, which can be treacherous and which might be shell middens of archaeological value. Avoid driving at night.

You can drive at greater speed on firm beach sand, but as a rule you should drive at a responsible speed and beware of anglers, children and other people.

Remember the beach is not a speedway. Do not fight your wheel when steering in soft sand; work with it. To exit from deep tracks, however, you should select a course, turn the wheel and power yourself out.

TIP: Don't forget your recovery kit!

DITCHES AND DONGAS: The secret here in most cases is to cross at an angle so that only one wheel at a time goes into the donga, which means at least three wheels have traction. Avoid cross-lifting of wheels.

Crossing requires great caution because if both wheels on one side of the vehicle slide into the donga, you are likely to get stuck and getting out is no easy task. Exiting dongas should also be done at an angle. The angled approach will give you extra 'lift' as opposed to a right-angled approach. Such a direct approach may cause a vehicle to break over and stick. A direct 'straight-on' approach may be required where conditions could cause cross-lifting of wheels.

ASCENTS AND DESCENTS: The key rule here is not to tackle hills at an angle because that invites a roll or slide.

ASCENTS

Check out the slope carefully before any ascent. If it is rocky, attack it at a lower speed to prevent losing traction when your wheels lift because of rocks. If the ascent seems smooth, you can attack it at a higher speed.

Engage four-wheel drive, and lock free-wheel hubs. Then select your gear according to the terrain. Accelerate a bit more as you begin the climb, but if the wheels start spinning, decelerate gently and accelerate again the moment your wheels stop spinning, but use your foot softly.

Don't be tempted to change gears during the climb and remember to ease off the accelerator as you reach the top – you never know what lies beyond the crest of the hill. Again common sense should always rule.

Tip: Learn cadence braking and practise this 'tap, tap' feathering on descents. This allows precise control and works in conjunction with compression braking.

Tip: The stall start. In case of a stall, which is common on a hill-climb, do not panic. First, gently engage your footbrake and handbrake to halt any backward slide. Then put the vehicle into reverse, hold the footbrake and remove your foot from the clutch. Next release the handbrake. The next step is to turn the ignition, start up the motor and release the footbrake at the same time. The engine will start and the vehicle should reverse safely down the hill against compression. Feather your brakes if necessary as you reverse.

TIP: Watch the front wheels as you restart. They should be in a straight line. Check your rearward route.

TIP: Learn the subtle difference between momentum and speed.

DESCENTS

The idea is to let the engine act as your brake to prevent a forward slide. Engage four-wheel drive, lock free-wheel hubs and select the lowest gear possible. Release the handbrake, let out the clutch and let the motor do the talking; the engine will act as your brake throughout the descent. Dependent on the gradient, you may have to cadence-brake to control your speed (feathering brakes with a light 'tap, tap' motion).

If your vehicle starts to slide to the side, don't use your brakes. Accelerate gently to regain control. Keep steering wheel straight at all times, and know the position of your front wheels. By the same token, don't try to change gear during a descent. If you depress the clutch, the vehicle could speed out of control down the hill.

TIP: If you stall, follow the stall-start procedure, but check that no obstacles such as ruts or rocks in front of your vehicle caused the stall.

DRIVING ON GRAVEL ROADS: This is stock-in-trade for 4x4's, but driver concentration needs to be high to avoid certain dangers, especially as many of these roads are travelled at speed. Drive in 4x4 high range for better traction and control. Chief among the dangers are soft sand on the verge of the road and gravel roads that slope downwards from the centre to the verges. In the case of the latter, vehicles must be

driven at an angle and hard braking or violent movement of the steering wheel should be avoided, as they could cause the vehicle to roll.

Another danger is stones and dust thrown up from oncoming or passing vehicles. The sensible driver will slow right down as will the courteous driver. Dust can be particularly deadly at speed because drivers' vision is impaired and they are often oblivious to obstacles or sharp turns ahead. The wise driver always negotiates gravel roads with their headlights on. Surface change on gravel roads can also be dangerous and sensitivity to this is vital.

Ruts and deep holes are common on gravel roads and usually present problems. However, if you see a deep rut in the road while you are travelling at speed, hit the brakes without locking them. Just before you hit the rut, accelerate over it. This should lift the front and save your suspension from damage.

Many gravel roads are badly corrugated, which can cause severe damage to a vehicle's suspension if taken at speed.

TIP: Wheelspin under any conditions causes loss of traction – back off the accelerator to regain traction. Ultimately wheelspin damages the environment and digs you in!

ROCKS: Many long stretches of rock exist off-road, often in rivers. Check such obstacles, bearing in mind the underside of your vehicle, diffs and transfer case – compare the size of the rocks to your ground clearance. Torque is important, so stay in a low gear and gently guide your vehicle to 'walk' over rocky terrain in low range. Once again, avoid cross-lifting wheels. With independent front suspension, lift is gained by putting a wheel on a rock as opposed to simply driving over it.

TIP: On average, your 4x4's clearance will allow you to drive over rocks about the size of a football.

SNOW: In light snow tyres will grip through the top surface or crust. Keep a steady speed and brake carefully. When in deep snow accelerate judiciously to avoid wheelspin. Be careful of building a wall of snow in front of your vehicle and be aware of possible hidden obstacles.

A FINAL WORD OF WARNING: Try to avoid driving in isolated areas and on bad roads at night. There is a high risk of accidents at night in off-road situations and out in the wilderness you might have great problems getting help in an emergency. The secret of success is to stick to daylight and to use your common sense at all times.

The golden rule of 4x4 driving is never to go in a single vehicle on an off-road excursion.

Recovery

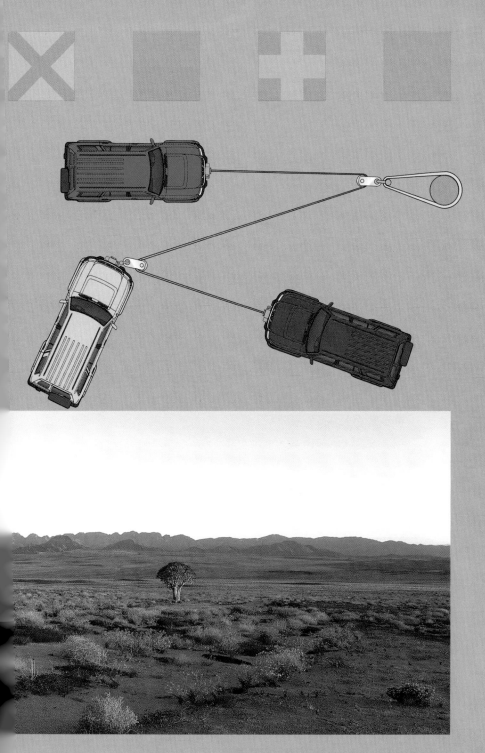

Recovery

Essential to recovery are the items of equipment needed. You should look at the route and terrain and ensure that the group travels with the right equipment. In the case of recovery straps there should be two kinetic straps of the same rating and one pull strap per three vehicles, a variety of rated alloy bow shackles and an emergency 3,5-metre four-ton tow strap.

You should ensure that you have adequate specialist recovery points on the front and rear of your vehicle, capable of handling the force of a recovery exercise. Their minimum breaking strain should be in excess of the strap or winch work load limit.

BASIC EQUIPMENT REQUIRED

JACKS: are essential, be they bottle jacks, air jacks or the high-lift variety. These are all covered in the tyre and accessory section.

RECOVERY KIT: the extent of your recovery kit is obviously determined by budget and whether a winch is fitted. A full kit will comprise the following:

SPADE: should be short and manoeuvrable with a pointed nose.

GLOVES.

SHACKLES.

SNATCH BLOCK.

PULL STRAP/WINCH CABLE EXTENSION (5–10 metres).

KINETIC STRAP (minimum 9 metres).

TOW STRAP (for long-distance towing 3,5-metre length in accordance with traffic regulations).

DRAG OR CHOKER CHAIN.

TREE PROTECTOR (3 metres).

FUNDAMENTALS

SHACKLES: It is a good idea to carry a variety of bow shackles as a larger variety may be needed to recover a heavier vehicle. Use rated alloy bow shackles, not commercial or D-shackles. The bow of the shackle has a larger inside working radius offering more room for attaching straps and more angled working ability if required. A rated shackle is easy to identify as the rating appears on the body and the pin is of a larger diameter than the body (the body and pin of a commercial shackle are of the same diameter).

When a shackle is tightened for recovery the pin should be loosened half a turn, as a shackle can 'tighten' due to the force of the recovery.

STRAPS: Common to the business are the pull or winch extension strap and the kinetic or snatch strap, both made of synthetic fibre, as well as the standard tow strap and the tree trunk protector.

PULL STRAP: Made of polyester with limited stretch, it is used to pull or tow lightly stuck vehicles through or over obstacles where a degree of control is required. Once securely attached to both vehicles, the recovery unit moves off at a moderate pace to effect recovery. Used as the first line of defence, movement should be gentle with as few jerks as possible. Pull straps can also be used to extend a winch cable.

KINETIC STRAP: Made of polyamide, most kinetic straps stretch 20–30% of their length. This is a short sharp elastic rebound and is used to extricate a severely bogged down unit from sand or mud. The strap is normally laid back over itself in an 'S' shape (about one and a half metres, or half of overall length). The recovery unit takes off normally in 2nd gear, low range in a straight line away from the stuck unit and stretches the strap to its fullest. Practice will allow a good driver to stop before the strap stops him, thereby allowing full utilisation of the kinetic capability and not straining the strap or recovery points on the vehicles. Sometimes this procedure may have to be repeated with a new rope, and if the vehicle is still partially stuck it may need to be winched.

Experienced off-roaders prefer to use a kinetic strap as a last line of defence due to its erratic nature.

TIP: Drivers should wear seatbelts at all times. A kinetic strap may in an emergency be used as a pull strap.

TREE TRUNK PROTECTOR: Protects the delicate bark of a tree when using a manual or electric winch, thereby providing a secure anchor point. Your tree trunk protector should be 100 mm wide, and 2–4 metres long.

- Keep bystanders clear in a recovery situation. All bystanders and those actively involved in a winching or pull/kinetic strap recovery should be at least twice the length of the strap or cable away from the vehicles.
- When straps have to be joined, do not use a shackle. The straps should be looped through one another with a branch placed between the two loops. This separates the loops. Otherwise, on stretching, the fibres would join, making it impossible to separate the two straps. Should straps snap, the branch would fall to the ground. A shackle could have been a potentially dangerous missile.

- Ideally straps having a same rating and function should be joined – in other words, do not join a snatch strap to a pull strap.

DO NOT JOIN WITH A D-SHACKLE   **JOIN STRAPS LIKE THIS**

Straps should be washed after use in sand or mud to remove abrasive particles. Thereafter they should be dried in shade as the fibre is sensitive to UV rays.

A strap from a reputable manufacturer should have a label stitched in detailing:

- Manufacturer.
- Material.
- Strength.
- Length.
- Application.
- Work load limit (laden vehicle mass).
- Factor of safety and/or minimum break strength.

NB: Without the above details, an unlabelled strap should be used only as a tow strap or thrown away. Your strap should be purchased in accordance with the vehicle you drive in terms of the work load limit. End loops should be well constructed with a loose, movable sleeve to prevent wear and tear and allow full protection.

KINETIC CAPABILITY

So often one sees multiple use of a strap. A good rule of thumb is that, after one rigorous snatch, the kinetic capability has been utilised and requires eight hours for every 10% of stretch to 'creep back' or be restored to its original length and kinetic capability, i.e. thus, to get back to 30% (full) extension requires 24 hours of rest.

The percentage of stretch is calculated according to the measured length of a strap. In other words, a 10% stretch on a 10-metre strap would be one metre. For example, when such a strap has stretched to 13 metres and no longer returns to its labelled length, it has lost its kinetic capibility. Strength has not been lost; it can be used as a pull strap in future.

TIP: There are two phases to the recovery of a strap: namely, the latent phase, which is over time, and an immediate phase on rebound, which restores a small portion of kinetic capability.

TIP: Important factors influencing kinetic capability:
- mass of the two units.
- how badly 'stuck' the unit to be recovered is.
- what traction is available to the recovering unit – in other words, the road surface.
- distance between vehicles and the speed at which the recovery unit moves.

NB: It assumed that when you travel in wilderness areas, you'll go with a companion. The reason is simple – it makes emergency situations so much easier to handle. Not only can the occupants of the second vehicle render assistance, but in the case of a complete write-off, or breakdown, the second 4x4 can transport you safely out of the wild. The first rule of survival is to stay with your vehicle. It is unwise to send one member or members of your party off to get help, unless it is to recce the immediate area.

WINCHING

You will be amazed to learn how many winch owners neglect to try out their equipment before they go travelling in the wild. We assume you are not one of these and that you have not only read the instruction book carefully, but have practised using your winch, loaded the cable and learned to 'listen' to your winch under various levels of strain. Discuss the concept of loading your winch cable with your dealer when installing a winch. Briefly, the procedure involves the tensioning of the cable onto the drum by using the winch under controlled conditions (i.e. winch your partner's car up a slight incline with the full cable). This will avoid future cable problems such as kinks and bends.

Remember, winches can be extremely dangerous as you are dealing with mechanical equipment and cable under severe strain.

A Few Tips for Safe Winching:

- Make sure bystanders are well clear of the winching area. As a rule of thumb, bystanders should keep away from the area extending from the winching vehicle to the point where the cable is attached. This is in case of a cable snap, which could cause the cable to whip around and injure bystanders in the cable's 'line of fire' (this distance should be twice the length of the extended cable).

- If the cable is under great strain, it is wise to dampen the cable at a point about $1/3$ of the length of the paid-out cable closest to the clevis hook (use a blanket, jacket or strap). In the event of a cable snap, the weight of the blanket will prevent the cable from whipping.
- When using a tree as an anchor point, always use a tree protector to prevent damage to the bark. The tree protector should be positioned close to the base of the tree.
- Use a cable guide to roll the cable onto the drum evenly.
- Always use winching gloves when handling cable. This will protect your hands from

burns and cuts from broken strands. Strong leather gardening gloves will do. Cuts heal slowly in the bush.

- Ensure that the winch cable is correctly attached to a sturdy towing eye or bow shackle and don't loop the cable back around connecting it onto itself, as this could damage it.
- Beware of loose clothing that might get caught up in the cable or snagged in the drum.
- Always ensure that there are at least five complete turns of cable left on the drum before winching, as the rope fastener will not support a heavy load.
- Never engage or disengage the clutch when there is a load on the winch.
- When using the winch to move a load, ensure that the winching vehicle's footbrake is depressed. This anchors the vehicle to the ground with all four wheels.
- Do not move the vehicle to assist the winch. The combination of the winch and the vehicle pulling together could overload the cable or the winch itself.

The winching procedure itself is quite straightforward. First secure the wheels of the winching or anchor vehicle. Ensure the cable is firmly attached to the damaged vehicle and begin to take up the slack. Before you put the cable under heavy strain, inspect its full length and all attachment points.

Try to avoid pulling at an angle as this creates drag and reduces the winch's pulling power. However, if you attach a snatch block, you can winch around corners while keeping the pull straight.

The long lead on the remote control will allow you to stand well clear. Your best position is behind the driver's door where you can control the engine's revs and brake, and have the necessary protection in case of a cable snap.

Whenever possible, use a snatch block and position the anchor vehicle at sufficient distance to be on firm ground.

Avoid running the winch at full power for a protracted period. You should pause frequently to cool the winch and allow the engine to recharge the battery (your winch should cool off if it becomes hot to the touch).

When you have successfully effected a winch recovery, your next step is to carefully examine the extent of damage to the vehicle.

Remember to take special note of the state of the underside and suspension which may have sustained damage. Do a routine check of oil, water and battery levels and see that you repack the vehicle properly before you set off.

TIP: Unload a heavily laden vehicle to reduce the strain on the winch.

SAFETY

- Never step over or stand close to a tensioned cable.
- Don't forget gloves.
- All vehicles should have adequate recovery points that draw off the chassis – both front and rear.
- Watch hands near the fairlead rollers and watch the control.
- Develop winch commands and work as a team, i.e.:
  OUT – a clockwise hand movement above your head.
  IN – an anti-clockwise hand movement at waist level.
  INTERMITTENT MOVEMENT OF CONTROL – open and close thumb and forefinger.
- Never winch with a frayed or badly kinked cable.
- When winching and using a bow shackle, the shackle pin should be at right angles to the direction of pull, otherwise the force can stretch the shackle, making it difficult to undo.

PROTECT YOUR WINCH CABLE WHEN WINCHING OVER AN OBSTACLE

- Never use your clevis hook as a strap attachment for recovery (mounting point). This could pull the cable into the roll, making it difficult to remove. **REMEMBER** maximum pulling power is on the last layer of cable on the drum and decreases as you add layers.
- For self-winching without an anchor point, a sand anchor, spare tyre (buried in the sand) or a steel stake can be used.

'CABLE SPLITTING'

Your snatch block can be used to re-route the direction of your winch cable, but its main function is 'doubling up'; simply put, this is when extra power is required (i.e. when you cannot run enough cable off your winch drum). You then 'split' the cable through a snatch block and back to the winch. This 'doubles' the power of your winch by giving you two lines pulling at the rated capacity, less about 10% for friction on the sheave (the enclosed wheel in the snatch block).

NB: This is only applicable when both lines run parallel. 'Doubling' also halves the line speed.

'DOUBLE-LINING'

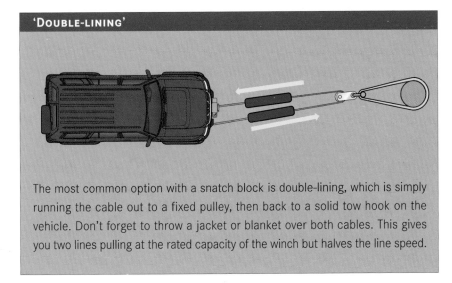

The most common option with a snatch block is double-lining, which is simply running the cable out to a fixed pulley, then back to a solid tow hook on the vehicle. Don't forget to throw a jacket or blanket over both cables. This gives you two lines pulling at the rated capacity of the winch but halves the line speed.

'TRIPLE-LINING'

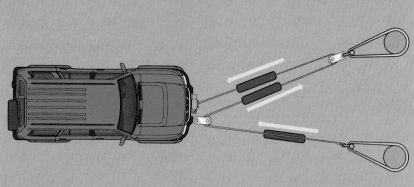

The next step is triple-lining, which will increase the power of your winch over a double-line setup. It also reduces line speed, but the increase in pulling power may make it worthwhile. In addition to needing a tow hook on your vehicle, triple-line rigging requires two snatch blocks and two anchors.

'TRIPLE-LINING' USING OTHER VEHICLES

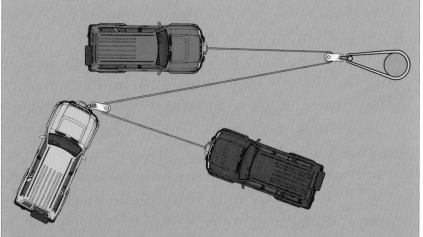

Here's another variation of the triple-line setup that also uses the angle-pulling technique from a second anchor on another vehicle. If you're able to reel out enough cable, your winch can rescue another 4x4 in just about any predicament, even when you can't get in line for a near-straight pull.

THE HAND WINCH

A hand winch is considerably cheaper than an electric unit. Obviously it is portable and can be used to the front or rear of a stuck vehicle. When not in use, the cable, handle and winch can be stored out of the way. The typical unit comes with a cable and a handle for winching in and out. Jaws in the winch grip move the cable as the handle is cranked. All safety methods should be followed and a snatch block may be used. To lengthen a cable, you can safely use a pull strap. A hand winch is a highly effective piece of equipment which requires a fair amount of manual effort – more than enough reason to improve your driving skills!

THE DRAG CHAIN

An often overlooked piece of recovery equipment. A drag chain consists of a length of rated, welded, steel-link chain with two removable clevis-type grab hooks able to link back over the chain and lock in place. Typical uses are:

- Where recovery points do not exist, the chain can be locked around the chassis on both sides to form an inverted 'V'. Recovery can be effected this way with both sides sharing the load.
- A section of chain can also be used for high-lift recovery if no high-lift point exists.
- The chain can be used to anchor off large rocks for recovery.
- Towing in emergency situations (as a last resort).

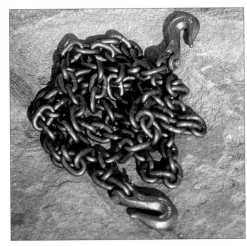

- The chain can be tied around obstacles such as trees which have to be moved. Do not use a strap for this as you are likely to chafe the webbing.

The minimum breaking strain should not be less than 8 000 kg and should have a minimum length of 3 metres.

THE MOST IMPORTANT SAFETY TIP

Never recover a vehicle using a towbar or bullbar that is not rated for the purpose. No strap should be placed over a towball. The galvanised ball and bolts may shear.

Only recover vehicles with a pin-type hitch if the bolts are high-tensile and of sufficient rating (breaking strain).

DRAWING ATTENTION

It may well be that you cannot recover the vehicle or you have badly injured passengers and cannot get back on track. Your only option is to try to draw attention to your predicament. Therefore it is important to have the necessary equipment with you.

CB radios have limited application in the wild, but cellphone technology has made communication possible through much of southern Africa's wilderness. In case these are not available, you might look to other methods of gaining attention (i.e. the more expensive satellite phones).

Flares should be standard equipment in the wilderness. Ships have to carry them by law and you would be wise to follow the navy's example. There are many different types of flares available on the market, such as hand-held smoke flares for daytime use and illumination flares for night use. The best, of course, are parachute flares which hang high and can be seen from a great distance and for a considerable time.

If you do not have flares, the vehicle's hooter is the obvious attention grabber, but a far more strident horn attached to an aerosol can is available for a few Rands.

Another obvious attention grabber is to light a fire. Keep the fire blazing by night and during the day, feeding it with damp grass to create smoke. On a clear, windless day your smoke path will be visible for miles around. Be sure to control your fire!

Remember, as a second and last reminder, don't leave your 4x4 vehicle.

EMERGENCY SPARES LIST
- Cable ties.
- Fan belt.
- Silicone spray (water repellent/lubrication).

- Tow rope.
- Wire – to tighten parts that have come adrift. (Bailing and fencing wire are also useful in improvising hose clamps).
- Jumper cables.
- Spare spark plugs.
- Engine oil, brake fluid and water.
- Insulation and duct tape.
- Tyre repair kit – tubeless.
- Tyre tube.
- Rubber bungees.
- Quickset epoxy.
- Tyre repair spray.
- A selection of pre-drilled flat bars which are useful to replace brackets, etc.
- A comprehensive tool kit with sockets, wrenches, spanners, screwdrivers, pliers, etc.

- Spare parts, depending on how far you travel from your vehicle's agents, should include items such as a computer box (engine management system), fuel filters, fan belts and radiator hoses.

TIP: A small hole in a fuel tank can be repaired by making a 'putty' from fine dust and soap shavings. Normal adhesives do not work as fuel is a 'solvent'.

Tyres and Accessories

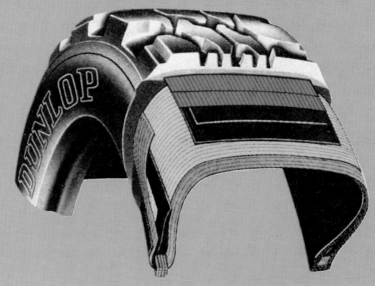

Tyres and Accessories

TYRES

TYRE TIPS

- Don't mix radial-ply with bias or cross-ply tyres on your vehicle. Always carry a pump, puncture repair kit and a good tyre pressure gauge.
- Fit metal valve caps with rubber seals to prevent foreign particles entering a valve.
- Understand your tyres' limits with regard to load as well as speed rating.
- Check wheel balance and alignment after protracted rough off-road travel.
- Carry two spades if possible.

Today we tend to run on radial-ply tyres, as they offer good traction, extended life and a passenger car-like ride on tar. The typical all-terrain multipurpose tyres brake well under most conditions and perform well off-road. Sidewall bulge was a problem with older radial-ply tyres, but nowadays light truck technology has resulted in a stronger and stiffer sidewall.

UNDERSTANDING YOUR TYRES

CONSTRUCTION

In a radial-ply tyre the body cords run in a radial direction across the tyre's circumference, from bead to bead. Cords are of nylon, polyester or rayon for steel-belted tyres. Breaker belts are made of steel cords and serve to brace and stabilise the tread in the road contact area. Radial cords, running as they do from bead to bead, reduce inner deformation in the shoulder and sidewalls.

A Typical Radial-ply Tyre's Construction

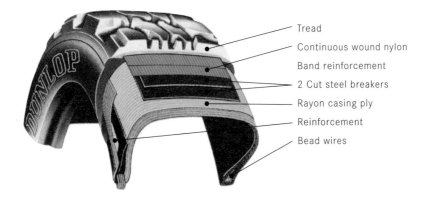

Tread

Continuous wound nylon

Band reinforcement

2 Cut steel breakers

Rayon casing ply

Reinforcement

Bead wires

The Sidewall

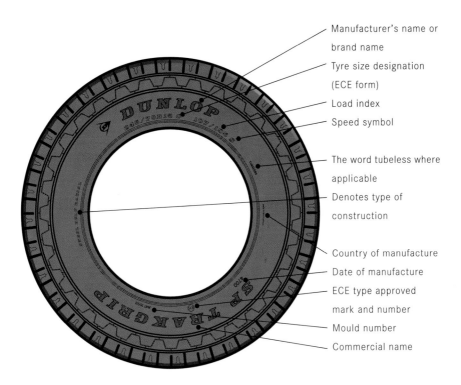

Manufacturer's name or brand name

Tyre size designation (ECE form)

Load index

Speed symbol

The word tubeless where applicable

Denotes type of construction

Country of manufacture

Date of manufacture

ECE type approved mark and number

Mould number

Commercial name

The Tyre's Sidewall Markings

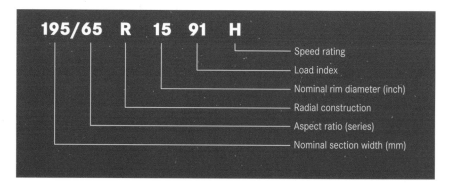

Following the rim diameter would be the load index and speed symbol.

The Load Index

Simply, this is an internationally recognised numerical code denoting the maximum load in kg that a tyre can carry at a specified km/h indicated by the speed symbol.

Speed Symbol

Tyres are produced to various speed ratings denoted by a speed symbol.

Tyre Speed Symbol Markings

Maximum Speed										
Speed symbol	L	M	N	P	Q	R	S	T	U	H	V
Speed (km/h)	120	130	140	150	160	170	180	190	200	210	240

NB: Many 4x4 accidents occur in open tar road conditions, where a combination of incorrect inflation, high speed and overloading cause heat build-up in the tyre. The heat build-up is caused by excessive deformation of the tyre and leads to destruction of the tyre components and a failure. It is wise to bear these factors in mind; if you are in any doubt, consult your tyre dealer.

Aspect Ratio

Aspect ratio is the ratio between the tyre's height from bead to crown and its width from sidewall to sidewall, expressed as a percentage.

BEAD

The bead is the part of the tyre that comes into contact with the wheel rim. Tyre beads are made of high-tensile steel and anchor the tyre to the rim.

FOOTPRINT

The footprint is the tread section that makes contact with the road surface.

SHOULDER

The shoulder of a tyre is the area where the tyre's sidewall and tread meet.

SIDEWALL

The sidewall is the side section of the tyre extending from the bead to the shoulder.

TREAD

The tyre's tread is the patterned surface section composed of cleats or lugs formulating the pattern or design. It is also the part of the tyre that comes in contact with the road surface. Various types of tread pattern exist to optimise the tyre's performance to suit various road or performance conditions such as AT – all terrain, MT – mud tyre, etc.

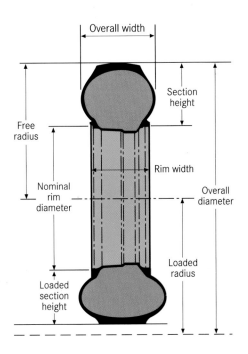

FLOTATION

Flotation is the tyre's ability to support a load under moving conditions across yielding terrain.

TYRE PRESSURE

Deflation is often controversial, yet an important technique that should be practised and implemented. Here are a few guidelines:

• Deflation improves traction but reduces ground clearance.
• Wheelspin with deflated tyres may cause the tyre to 'debead', that is to come off the rim. This may happen in rocky or sandy conditions.

- Tyres should be deflated when cold, not hot (hot air expands and gives higher tyre pressure readings). You could unseat a tyre from its rim when it cools down.
- In rough terrain, deflation also allows tyres to absorb more shock.
- In rocky terrain, deflated tyres can mould themselves to rocks as they go over them.

TIP: If you are forced to deflate hot tyres, add at least 0,5-bar as a precaution against 'debeading'.

SAND: Lower pressure to increase traction. It is worthwhile to deflate the front tyres only, as this will compress the sand for the back tyres to ride over. As hot sand has little moisture, it is looser and more difficult to drive on.

WATER: Do not lower pressure in water as obstacles under water may not be visible. It also lowers the vehicle's clearance.

ROCKS: Whilst deflation allows better grip, be careful not to spin or pinch a softer tyre as this could unseat the tyre or damage the sidewall.

MUD: Slightly lower pressure will increase the surface area and improve flotation, but beware of hidden obstacles.

TIP: Modern 4x4 tyres are designed to be used at the recommended pressure under most conditions. Use deflation as a last resort to overcome severe conditions. Reinflate tyres as soon as possible. Select your tyres according to the road conditions where most vehicle usage takes place. It is important to consider the following factors: size, width (this has an influence on flotation) and load/speed rating.

Accessories

Fire Extinguishers

No vehicle should be without a reasonably sized general purpose fire extinguisher. Dangerous situations related to the vehicle as well as general campsite problems could arise and a fire extinguisher will prove to be invaluable. This item of equipment should always be readily available.

Winches and Recovery Equipment

The most common winches are electronic drum winches mounted to the front of a vehicle. These are relatively expensive items, which in many cases are not extensively utilised. Prior to fitting a winch you should be aware of its potential in a recovery situation and assess this in the light of your destinations. Once you have fitted a winch you should assemble a recovery kit which would typically comprise:

- Snatch block.
- Bow shackles.
- Tree protector.
- Pull strap/kinetic strap.
- Cable guide.
- Leather gloves.

Bog Mats and Sand Ladders

Mats, ladders and tracks are placed in front of a vehicle to guide traction when a vehicle has bogged down. They are a much cheaper recovery option than a winch, but may in many cases be equally useful in a recovery situation.

JACKS

There are primarily three jacking options available to the off-roader. Prior to purchasing a jack, you should become familiar with the operation as well as its suitability to your vehicle.

Bottle Jacks

These are hydraulic or worm-drive jacks which are supplied with most vehicles. Familiarise yourself with the jacking points for this type of jack – as a rule of thumb, the jack should be rated 3 times in excess of your vehicle's weight.

Air Jacks

A relatively new option available to the off-roader, the air jack is a PVC bag which is inflated by exhaust gas through a flexible pipe to lift a vehicle. This is also an extremely useful item of equipment to assist in righting a vehicle which has rolled onto its side. You should carry large cable ties or a quick release clamp to secure the flexible hose to the exhaust.

High-Lift Jacks

An arguably indispensable tool, but one with a dubious reputation. A vehicle requires strong jacking points – in many cases gussets would have to be welded to the chassis to facilitate the use of a high-lift jack. The jack has a variety of other uses in recovery situations, but a great deal of practice is required prior to using a high-lift jack in a real situation as it can also be a dangerous piece of equipment.

PLATES

Bases are required for all jacks. In the case of bottle and high-lift jacks they provide a stable jacking platform and could be as simple as a 30x30 cm square board. An air jack would require a plywood base to protect it from being punctured by stones or thorns in more remote areas.

JERRY CANS/LONG-RANGE TANKS

Long-range tanks are now available for most vehicles and can greatly extend their range. As an option they are preferable to jerry cans as they are safer and less of a security risk. As a safety measure, a jerry can should be fitted and only filled when you know that fuel may not be readily available.

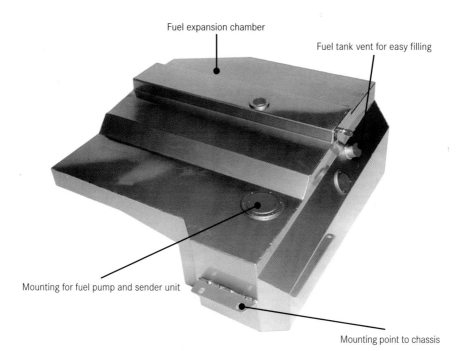

Fuel expansion chamber

Fuel tank vent for easy filling

Mounting for fuel pump and sender unit

Mounting point to chassis

GRILL AND AIR INTAKE NETS

When travelling long distances over grasslands, seeds and husks accumulate on a radiator, greatly reducing its cooling ability. They are also extremely irritating when coming through the air intake into the cabin. Nets can be purchased from specialist off-road shops, but adequate nets can be made using hail netting secured to your bullbar with cable ties and held in place over your intakes with duct tape. Do not use mosquito netting, wire mesh, electrical tape, masking or packing tape – they won't work!

SNORKELS

Snorkels are invaluable accessories as they enable a vehicle to breathe clean air when travelling in dusty conditions, thereby enhancing engine efficiency. Snorkels are also useful for the increase they bring about in wading depth.

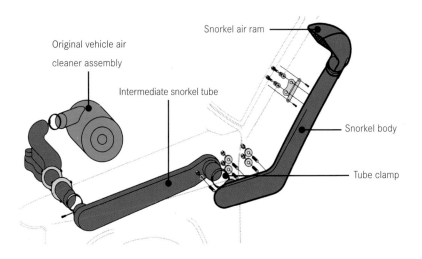

Snorkel air ram

Original vehicle air cleaner assembly

Intermediate snorkel tube

Snorkel body

Tube clamp

ANCHORS

A variety of anchors are available for recovery situations where the vehicle is stuck on a beach or in sand. They obviate the need to bury a spare tyre and thus provide a winching point. Substantial stakes may also be driven into hard earth to provide an anchoring point when one does not exist.

PUMPS

Another indispensable piece of equipment, especially if tyres are deflated to traverse soft sand and have to be reinflated afterwards.

Pumps vary from simple foot and manual upright options to compressors and sophisticated pumping systems. A pump is essential, but the type chosen would be determined by your budget and level of physical fitness (manual pumps require considerable physical exertion).

DRIVING LIGHTS

If any of your expeditions involve night driving, good spotlights are important. In remote areas, people and animals (both wild and domestic) are a constant danger. Your lights should be totally waterproof if you intend to ford rivers or other water courses.

ROOF RACKS

A variety of roof racks, designed to provide additional packing space, is available. Many of them are custom-built options. Roof racks may be aluminium, steel, or steel and timber. 'All metal' roof racks do have drawbacks in that they will 'chafe' items packed onto them, no matter how well secured. Timber, however, requires ongoing maintenance and treatment. Racks are extremely useful as they provide a base for a rooftop tent and can be used to carry spare tyres, fuel and bulky equipment. The platform can also

be used for game viewing and photography. A word of caution, however. Pay careful attention to the distribution of weight as the last thing you need is to overload a vehicle's front or rear suspension. Packing a load high also plays havoc with a vehicle's centre of gravity and could result in the vehicle rolling! Your heavy items should be packed lower down inside the vehicle. A high load also has a negative influence on fuel consumption as a result of an increase in aerodynamic drag.

TRAILERS

A full chapter could be devoted to the purchase of a trailer. Once again, budget plays an important part. A few worthwhile points to consider are:

- Braking capability.
- Compatible tyre size (common spare tyre).
- Matching tyre tracking width.
- Suitable suspension.
- Fitment of mudflaps.
- Packing capability.
- Tie-downs inside and storage compartments.

The list is endless, but more and more off-road trailers are coming onto the market – evaluate the various options for total suitability before finally purchasing a trailer.

FRIDGES AND COOLER BOXES

The ability to keep food and drinks cool for the duration of a trip is a luxury worth considering. A variety of fridges is available, which will necessitate the fitting of a dual-battery split-charge system. As the compressor is linked to a thermostat, they are relatively efficient in terms of the amount of current that they draw. Cooler boxes, if correctly used, have the ability to cool items – in many cases for up to a week. The trick here is to pack plenty of frozen items, ice bricks and loose ice and not to open the cooler more often than is absolutely necessary.

If your travels call for regular use of coolers, it will be worthwhile to invest in the more expensive 'steel-belted' options; they are more durable with better cooling properties. Coolers should be protected from scavengers if left out at night. Hyenas have been known to totally destroy 'steel-belted' coolers to get at the contents.

BULLBARS/OFF-ROAD BUMPERS

These are for serious off-road conditions requiring maximum approach and departure angles, winch fitment, jacking points and recovery points. Steel front and rear bumpers are available. Fitment should be carried out by a specialist dealer and items should be recommended by the vehicle manufacturer. High-tensile steel bolts with 'Nylock' nuts should be used, rather than the galvanised variety.

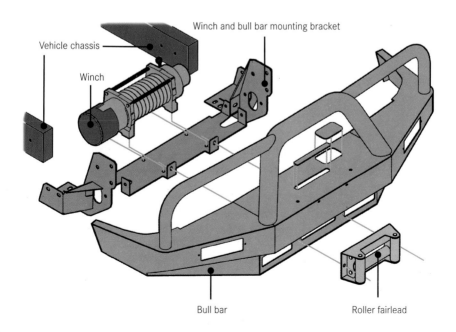

Winch and bull bar mounting bracket

Vehicle chassis

Winch

Bull bar

Roller fairlead

Repairs

Repairs

Apply the old adage 'prevention is better than cure'. Prior to embarking on a trip have your vehicle serviced by your dealer in accordance with its servicing schedule and the **4-point off-road check**.

The **4-point off-road check** covers the following areas which are critical to the performance of your vehicle and to the ultimate enjoyment of your trip.
- Mechanical and electrical.
- Suspension.
- Transmission.
- Wheels and tyres.

MECHANICAL AND ELECTRICAL
- Oil change.
- Engine analysis, fuel and electrical system.
- Replace oil and fuel filters (in the case of a diesel unit , fitting of an extra water trap and fuel filter will obviate problems caused by contaminated diesel).
- Inspect all 'V' belts.
- Pressure-test and check radiator and all hoses; if necessary flush, clean and refill, not forgetting coolant/antifreeze.
- Check engine and gearbox mounts.
- Check electrical system:
  - spotlights
  - spare batteries/charging systems
  - winch and winch cable (check operation, winch control and water damage).
- Check brake fluid.

- Check battery fluid level.
- Check windscreen washer fluid level.

SUSPENSION

- Check shock absorbers and coil springs, upgrade to gas shocks if necessary.
- Check leaf springs, shackle bolts and bushes.
- Check and adjust torsion bars.
- Check wheel balance/alignment.
- Carry out general inspection of chassis, nuts, bolts, brackets, 'U' bolts, etc.

TRANSMISSION

- Change oil in gearbox/transfer box and differentials.
- Check all seals and plugs.
- Check breather pipes on differentials if fitted or locate breathers for closure if using vehicle for extended periods in water.
- Check driveshaft universal couplings and fastenings.

WHEELS AND TYRES

- Check rims (steel or alloy) for damage.
- Check tyres, tread, sidewalls, valves, etc. for wear or damage (do not forget the spare wheel).
- Check brakes, hydraulic fluid, brake leads, cables, discs, drums, pads, shoes, etc. (and do not neglect load sensors).
- Check bearings and free-wheeling hubs for water damage, lubrication and function).
- Check that you have selected the correct tyre for the application, i.e. sand, mud, shale, rocks, etc. All tyres must be of the same circumference.

Tools and Emergency Items

Tools

- Do not forget the basic small tools, jack wheel spanner, pump and your emergency kit. The emergency kit is covered in the packing guide, but you should develop your own kit.

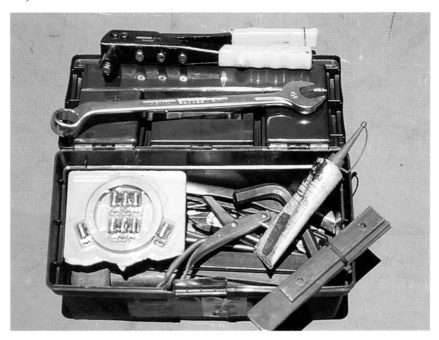

Spares

Obviously, your destination and the type of vehicles in your group will determine your requirements – avoid duplication and split your requirements amongst your fellow off-roaders. Many dealers will offer to refund you for spares purchased from them, if you return them after a trip in their original packaging and condition.

Running Repairs

Despite having serviced and checked your vehicle, a variety of emergencies may arise while in the bush. Your emergency kit and ingenuity will often be all that is required to get you going.

Rough terrain can puncture fuel tanks and drain plugs can also drop out. Ensure that you carry spare oil if you are far from civilisation and have an adequate supply of cork, leather and self-tapping screws to effect makeshift repairs.

Baling wire will enable you to clear blocked fuel lines, clamp and repair broken hoses and splice rods and bars to repair leaf springs in an emergency.

Improvisation is the name of the game. Utilising ingenuity and available material will keep you on the road until you can purchase the necessary replacement parts or reach a service centre.

ON YOUR RETURN

You should steam-clean your engine, chassis, suspension, etc. as soon as possible, to remove accumulated mud and dust, thereby enabling a visual inspection.

Bear in mind that extensive sand travel may make it necessary to have torsion bars and wheel alignment reset. Water and mud with fine silt particles can play havoc with clutches, starter motors and brakes. Radiator cores may also become blocked, affecting the cooling capability. Immediately check for water in transmission, transfer case and differentials. Oil may have to be changed whilst on a trip.

TIP: Oil that is water-contaminated takes on a milky white colour.

Basic Survival

Basic Survival

BASIC SURVIVAL HINTS

It all boils down to survival of the fittest and in this case, to the level of mental agility required to cope with an emergency should the need arise. Certain basics will help you to cope with most situations. A few of these will be explored below.

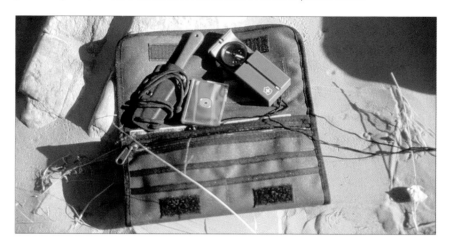

BASIC SURVIVAL KIT

An emergency can arise at any time, even if you are driving on a National Road, heading for a coastal resort. You should always carry the following items with you, some of which have already been covered.

- Tool kit.
- Tow rope.
- Tyre repair kit.
- Duct tape/cable ties.
- Wire.
- Assorted nuts, bolts and washers.
- Fan belt.
- Pre-drilled flat bars.
- Survival kit/first aid kit.
- Knives – essential to any trip are your knives, which can be very useful. The choice of knives is extremely personal, but two knives should be used:
  Heavy knife – this can serve a variety of purposes and can even cut wood or kindling. Ghurka-style knives are now available at camping suppliers and are extremely versatile.
  Small knife – the pocket or penknife can handle all the tasks which are too small

for your heavy knife. The lock-blade versions tend to be safer. Multipurpose tools are also worth taking on trips as they perform many functions.

Keep your knife sharp and sheathed if not in use.

- Signals – a situation could arise when some form of signal may be needed, either to warn others of danger or to attract a search and rescue party. Always include the following items:
  - Warning triangle.
  - Mirror.
  - Torch.
  - Fire starter.
  - Emergency flares.

Communication in an emergency situation when in a remote environment could rely on light from a mirror, a torch or ground-to-air signals. The following two tables will be helpful in a rescue situation.

GROUND-TO-AIR SIGNALS

These simple signals will enable you to attract the attention of an aircrew and communicate with them. They can be constructed by using rocks, logs or a combination thereof or scratched out in the sand with a shovel (the last option being the least legible).

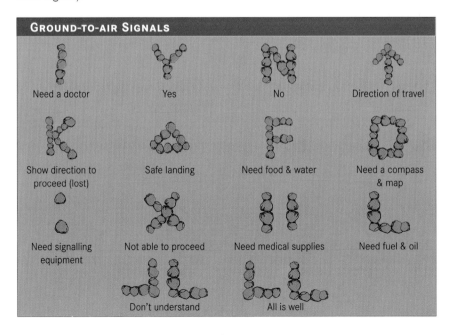

GROUND-TO-AIR SIGNALS

Need a doctor	Yes	No	Direction of travel
Show direction to proceed (lost)	Safe landing	Need food & water	Need a compass & map
Need signalling equipment	Not able to proceed	Need medical supplies	Need fuel & oil
	Don't understand	All is well	

MORSE CODE

You can send morse code by radio, torch or whistle (also by heliograph or smoke). Bear in mind that for an amateur it is easier to transmit morse than to receive it. 'HELP' is: 3-short, 3-long, 3-short (SOS – Save Our Souls) in morse code.

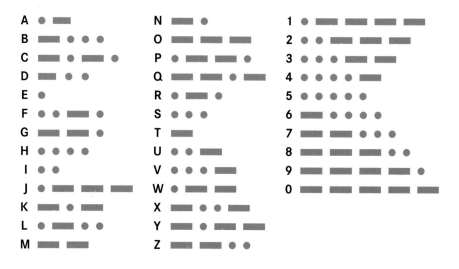

SOS

A A A A A A (I have a message)

T T T T   (I am receiving you)

R   (Roger/Yes)

WATER

The importance of carrying an ample supply of water cannot be overemphasised. Depending on a variety of factors such as the level of exertion, temperature, diet and weather, an average adult will consume at least 1,5 litres per day. The effects of water loss without replacement vary from thirst through headaches and dizziness to delirium and, in extreme cases, death. Should you run out of water or be stranded, the following methods of water collection are useful.

RAIN COLLECTION

When in camp or if stranded, set out containers to collect rainwater. Flow from shelters can also be directed into containers. A waterproof groundsheet pegged down a slope can also channel water. Rainwater will not require purification.

PLANTS

Plants give off water vapour which can be collected by enclosing the leaves in a plastic bag and channelling the vapour into a small container.

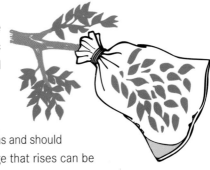

DIGGING

Water often seeps in marshy or muddy areas and should you dig a hole into the ground the seepage that rises can be purified and drunk – don't dig where the area smells or where a layer of surface scum is present. This water will need boiling or purification.

CONDENSATION

In the desert, condensation can be your saviour as it may be the only way to obtain life-sustaining moisture. A solar still can be constructed very simply, enabling you to collect water. The temperature difference between two surfaces causes air to heat up and become saturated. Condensation takes place on the coolest surface. A hole roughly one metre wide and 60 cm deep should be dug. Put a container in the bottom and, if at all possible, surround it with moist soil or undrinkable water (i.e. urine or sea water – not in the container). Then spread a plastic sheet over the hole and either peg in place or weight it down with rocks. The centre of the sheet should be weighted over the container with a fist-sized rock. As water vapour condenses on the inside of the sheet it will run down into the container. The procedure can be used to condense sea water using a plastic bowl of sea water and a mug.

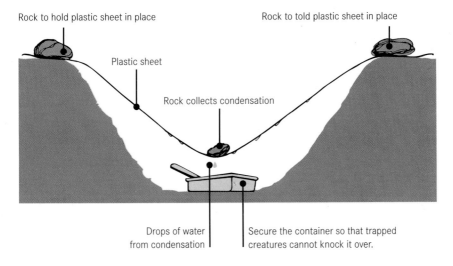

Rock to hold plastic sheet in place

Rock to told plastic sheet in place

Plastic sheet

Rock collects condensation

Drops of water from condensation

Secure the container so that trapped creatures cannot knock it over.

PURIFICATION

Most wild water sources will require purification and filtration. Investigate all methods and, depending on your destination, decide on your particular requirement. Although iodine, chlorine tablets and potassium permanganate are useful in an emergency situation, it is often better to purchase a purification system from your outdoor supplier. The more expensive systems are used throughout the world and require no chemical additives. In an absolute emergency you can filter water through a suitable piece of material (sock, cloth or pantihose) prior to purification by boiling.

DIRECTION

If you are without a compass there are a few simple methods you can use to find direction. A good deal of fun can be had simply by exploring them. We have all learnt that the sun rises in the east and sets in the west – this in fact can be used as a simple indicator of direction. Use the sun to orient yourself and find approximate direction simply by using an analog watch or alarm clock. In the southern hemisphere, point the 12 o'clock mark at the sun – north will be roughly halfway between the sun and the hour hand.

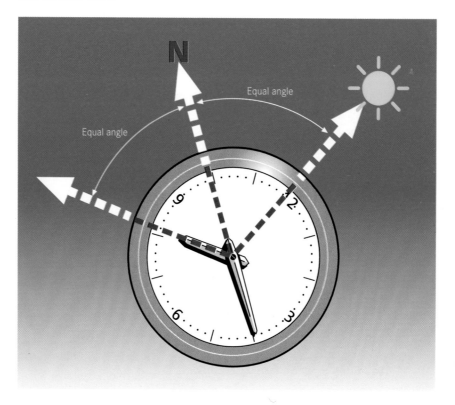

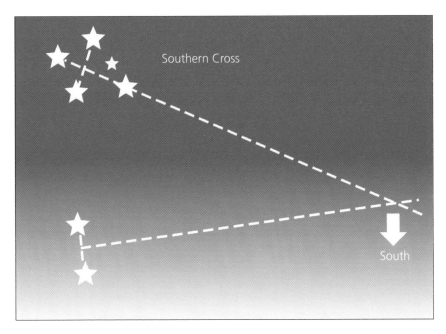

At night you can use the Southern Cross to help you. Create an imaginary line from the long axis of the cross about 4,5 times its length and a bisecting line from the two bright stars below the cross (slightly to the right); approximate due south will be on the horizon – perpendicular to the point where the two lines bisect.

TRAVEL MEDICINE BASICS

- The most common journey-disrupting illness suffered by all travellers irrespective of style of travel, status or destination is traveller's diarrhoea.
- The most common cause of death in travellers under the age of 40 is trauma or accidents.
- The most common cause of death in travellers over the age of 40 years is cardio-vascular disease.
- The most serious, life-threatening disease in travellers in Africa is malaria.
- The most common vaccine-preventable disease in travellers to developing countries is hepatitis A, more commonly known as jaundice.
- The only compulsory vaccine for travellers in Africa is that for yellow fever and only for those travellers to and from yellow fever-endemic countries. This is a stipulation of the International Health Regulations of the World Health Organisation.

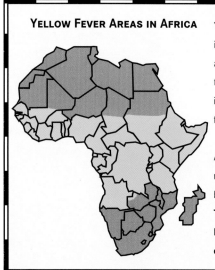

YELLOW FEVER AREAS IN AFRICA

Yellow fever is caused by a virus transmitted by infected mosquitoes and is potentially fatal. Travellers are required by law to have the vaccination when travelling to/from infected countries. The vaccine is only valid ten days after innoculation and lasts for ten years.

A traveller without a valid vaccination certificate may be refused entry into an infected country and be placed under quarantine on return to South Africa. **The vaccine may only be obtained from Department of Health-approved vaccination centres.**

- The yellow fever vaccination certificate is only valid ten days after administration – get yours in time – and is available only from Department of Health-licensed yellow fever centres. This is usually a travel clinic or your nearest District Surgeon.
- Cholera vaccination is no longer required from anyone, in accordance with the World Health Organisation. A cholera vaccination exemption stamp may, however, be useful at some borders.
- Routine, childhood vaccinations should all be up to date. Make sure that you have had a tetanus (lockjaw) booster in the last five years; if not, get one prior to departure

or even if you are staying at home. Tetanus bacteria exist in soil everywhere and you may even contract it in your own backyard. The vaccine is inexpensive and the disease potentially lethal. Having a booster prior to departure removes the need to seek medical attention for minor cuts and scratches on safari.

- Travel medical insurance is of the utmost importance for all travellers – even inside South Africa. Medical care may be substandard in some places, is charged in US dollars everywhere in the rest of Africa and repatriation back to South Africa, even from neighbouring states, will cost thousands of dollars (consult the AA, your insurance broker, a travel agent or travel clinic about cover).
- Pre-hospital emergency services are rudimentary or non-existent in most areas in Africa. Do not expect speedy or efficient paramedics to rush to you in the event of an emergency. The correct approach to this problem is not to stock an extensive first aid kit but to prevent accidents and injury in the first place by heeding the basic rules to avoid injury.

Basic Rules to Avoid Injury

- Always wear a seat belt; do not drive faster than the terrain will allow.
- Do not drink and drive.
- Do not drive when tired.
- Do not drive at night in rural areas.
- Do not act irresponsibly by diving into unknown waters or scaling heights unless you have the correct training, equipment and back-up.
- Do not attempt difficult river crossings late in the day.
- Don't travel alone in the bush.
- Establish where the nearest reliable ambulance service or medical centre may be when planning your trip.

Emergency First Aid

Cardio-Pulmonary Resuscitation

Adequate training in CPR is a must as there is no other condition requiring more immediate attention than heart arrest or breathing failure. Tissue damage becomes likely if the heart and lungs are not restarted within four minutes. Not knowing CPR could have fatal consequences.

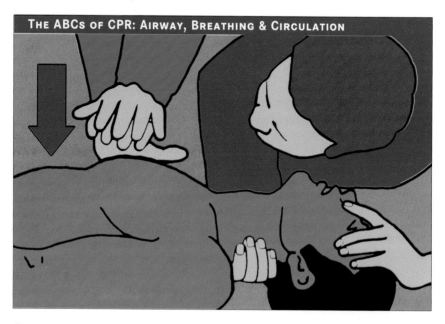

The ABCs of CPR: Airway, Breathing & Circulation

Choking

Choking occurs when a foreign body has lodged either fully or partially in the airway (trachea). Partial obstruction will result in severe coughing (which may dislodge the object), while full obstruction causes breathing to cease and the victim to display the 'universal distress signal' – grasping of the throat with the fingers and thumb. First aid training should adequately cover the 'Heimlich' manoeuvre and other ways of restoring breathing.

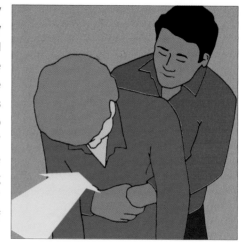

BLEEDING

Three types of bleeding exist namely:

EXTERNAL Blood escaping as a result of an injury or wound – can be capillary, venous or arterial.

SUBCUTANEOUS Within tissue and muscle as a result of a bump or injury with a blunt instrument – can result in bruising and swelling.

INTERNAL As a result of trauma or illness – in some cases patients may cough or vomit up blood or pass blood in stool. The latter may be bright red or black.

Bleeding ceases in response to direct pressure and application of a dressing, pressure pad or bandage (clean cloth will do in an emergency). Maintain pressure and elevate the affected limb above the level of the patient's heart until bleeding ceases. In the case of internal bleeding, loss of blood is not always visible, but the patient is likely to display signs of shock (pallor, temperature loss, clamminess and a rapid, weak pulse). The patient should be kept warm until help arrives. Small sips of water may be administered or lips may be moistened.

BROKEN BONES

A fracture is a break in the bone as a result of a direct or indirect force. Any movement thereafter will cause severe pain. Administer a painkiller, if available, prior to immobilising the damaged limb. Immobilising will stabilise the fracture

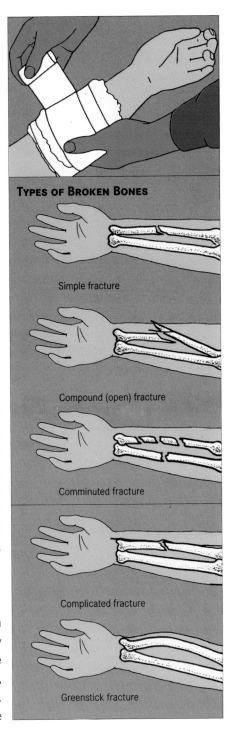

TYPES OF BROKEN BONES

Simple fracture

Compound (open) fracture

Comminuted fracture

Complicated fracture

Greenstick fracture

prior to administering medical aid; it will serve to prevent further pain and complications. If in doubt, treat the injury as a fracture and leave the final evaluation to a doctor. Always check circulation distal (hand or foot end of the limb) to the fracture.

MOVING A CASUALTY

This should only be resorted to when competent medical help is not readily available or the source of danger cannot be moved away from the patient. Except in the case of a facial injury, patients should be suitably immobilised prior to being moved. Be as gentle as possible and use as many helpers as are available to avoid aggravation of an injury. Techniques for placing a patient on a stretcher, such as 'log rolling', should be learnt and practised as spinal injuries require simultaneous movement of the head, torso and limbs.

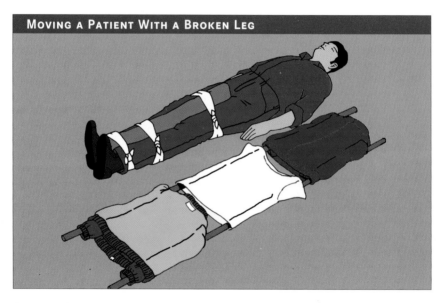

MOVING A PATIENT WITH A BROKEN LEG

Assume that all trauma victims have a spinal injury until proven otherwise by X-ray examination.

TRAVELLER'S DIARRHOEA

At least 25% of travellers suffer from traveller's diarrhoea. The most likely cause will be the consumption of contaminated food or water with bacteria that occur locally but do not always cause illness (*E. coli*). Traveller's diarrhoea is self-limiting in the majority of cases and a specific cause need only be sought if it persists. It is important to replenish lost fluids to counter the resultant dehydration. Food should be avoided and clear fluid or rehydration solutions ('Electropak') should be taken.

PREVENTION

- Cook it, peel it or leave it is the rule.
- Drink only bottled or boiled/purified water or sealed fizzy drinks.

TREATMENT

- The first 24 hours, rehydrate with clean water and oral rehydration solution.
- If diarrhoea persists for longer than 24 hours, take 'loperamide' in accordance with the instructions (two tablets immediately, then one after each loose stool to a maximum of six tablets in 24 hours).
- If diarrhoea persists after another 24 hours, consider an antibiotic such as Ciprofloxacine, Doxycycline or Co-trimoxazole.
- If a fever persists or there is blood or mucus in the stools, see a doctor as soon as possible.

BURNS

In the bush, burns are primarily caused by contact with heat sources such as steam, a fire, a hot pot or even an engine manifold.

Burns are traditionally classified as 1st, 2nd or 3rd degree, but can also be evaluated as 'superficial' or 'deep'. Immediately immerse a burn in cold water or cover with a clean wet dressing. This will help prevent tissue damage. Thereafter the burn should be dressed and protected to avoid infection. Clean, lint-free dressing, paraffin gauze or burnshield can be applied to burns that cover a large area. In most cases, burns are the result of negligence.

HEATSTROKE

Generally the result of over-exertion in the hot sun. A hat and protective clothing should be worn. The level of exertion should be evaluated according to age and fitness. A suitable sunscreen should cover all unprotected areas and water should

be drunk regularly. Sure signs that someone has heatstroke are feverishness, incoherence, vomiting, cessation of sweating and unconsciousness. The victim should be placed in a cool, shady spot and gradually cooled through the removal of clothing and bathing with cool water. The victim can also be fanned. On no accounts should a victim be immersed in cold water. Severe heatstroke can be fatal, so preventive measures are essential.

TICK-BITE FEVER

Two different types of ticks are found in bush and long grass or on domestic animals. Tick-bite fever occurs in two forms, an urban and a less severe rural form. Ticks attach themselves to the legs, arms and exposed bodies of passing animals and people as they brush past. Tick-bite fever will develop within days of being bitten by a tick infected with *Rickettsia conorii* or *africae*.

TICK

PREVENTION

- Wear long-sleeved shirts and long pants.
- Soak bush clothing in a synthetic pyrethroid ('Peripel', 'Permacote' or 'Bayticol') for a few minutes and dry flat a few days prior to departure.
- Apply a DEET-containing insect repellent to exposed skin areas before walking in the bush.
- When returning from a walk, carefully examine your body for ticks.
- Add a cap of paraffin to bath water when returning; this will kill ticks on your body.

SYMPTOMS

The incubation period lasts for four to fourteen days. The initial symptoms are a fever, severe headache, muscle and joint pains and sensitivity to light. Tick-bite fever presents itself just like a severe flu – or even malaria. An ulcer with a hard black centre may be found on the skin where the bite occurred. Glands in the area may be swollen and a rash may also appear on the torso, arms and legs or even on the palms of the hands. Pneumonia and heart inflammation are possible complications of the bite.

TREATMENT

The victim should be kept at rest in subdued light. Codeine or paracetamol will provide relief from headache. The condition responds rapidly to treatment with either tetracycline or erythromycin. Although mostly self-limiting, it is sometimes fatal in the very young, very elderly or debilitated.

SNAKE BITES

In Africa snake bites are relatively uncommon and fatalities are rare. Most bites can be avoided by being alert when in grassy or forested areas. Wear high boots and take care when climbing or clambering over rocks.

The majority of snakes are not poisonous; however, the ones that are can be categorized as follows:

NEUROTOXIC

Cause paralysis of the respiratory muscles that may rarely cause death within minutes. Onset of symptoms usually within minutes. The symptoms include: eye muscle weakness, speech impairment and difficulty in swallowing. Respiratory paralysis usually only develops after a few hours. The bite itself may not be very painful or swollen. Mambas, rinkhals and cobras (non-spitting) are typical of this group.

CYTOTOXIC

Cause massive tissue destruction that may lead to death after days if not treated correctly. Local pain and swelling of the limb often within minutes of the bite. Puffadder and gaboon viper are examples of this group. These types of snakes are responsible for about 90% of dangerous snake bites as they are 'lazy' and do not move away as you approach, rather striking out as you are about to step on them.

GREEN MAMBA

RINKHALS

CAPE COBRA

PUFFADDER

GABOON VIPER

Haemotoxic

Cause a general bleeding disorder that starts a few hours after the bite. The boomslang and the vine or twig snake fall into this group. These snakes are very rarely the cause of dangerous snake bites as they are shy, seldom encountered and are back-fanged.

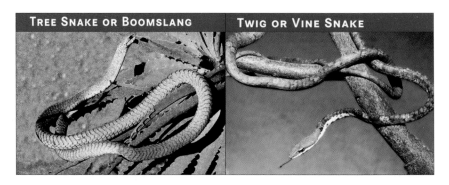

| TREE SNAKE OR BOOMSLANG | TWIG OR VINE SNAKE |

You should learn the technique of pressure-immobilisation of a snake bite: apply a pressure dressing over the bite and a crepe bandage from just above the fingers (in order to monitor perfusion) to the top of the limb, and then splint the arm or leg. Transport the victim on a stretcher to minimize the absorption of the venom.

Do not cut the wound, suck venom or apply a tourniquet. Seek immediate medical assistance and begin artificial respiration if respiratory paralysis becomes evident.

Snake anti-venom may be life-saving in the event of serious bites. There is a polyvalent anti-venom for neuro- and cytotoxic bites and a special one for haemotoxic bites.

The anti-venom should be stored properly and administered intravenously under direct medical supervision – it is seldom practical to include it in a first aid kit.

Rabies

Rabies is caused by a virus and is lethal once the patient becomes symptomatic. It is endemic in much of Africa and occurs in wild as well as domestic animals.

A rabies vaccine is available and effective provided that a full course had been correctly administered either before or after exposure to an infected animal bite, a scratch or lick over broken skin or mucosa. It is expensive and should not be necessary if common sense procedures are followed. The pre-exposure rabies vaccination (a series of three injections over a two- to four-week period) is NOT advised.

PREVENTION

- Avoid all contact with domestic and wild animals as far as possible.
- Consider **ALL** animals encountered as potentially rabid.

MANAGEMENT OF A SUSPECTED RABID ANIMAL INJURY

- Wash the wound immediately under lots of running water.
- Do not scrub the wound to avoid forcing the virus into the injured tissue.
- Apply a dressing containing iodine.
- **The victim must be vaccinated within 24–48 hours from the time of the bite – vaccination must not be deferred to the end of the journey.**
- The source of the vaccine must be reliable – a reputable manufacturer and strict maintenance of the cold chain must be ensured, as well as the correct administration.
- In some instances rabies immuneglobuline must be given simultaneously.
- A full course of immunisation must be completed to ensure efficacy.
- If you are uncertain regarding the correct treatment of a suspected rabies bite, you should consult your travel doctor or travel medical insurance company immediately.

CORRECT FIRST AID MANAGEMENT IN ALL SITUATIONS

- Keep the patient still and calm (as well as the first aider!).
- Bandage and apply a splint to the injured limb.
- Get to the nearest medical facility.

Spiders and scorpions are found all over southern Africa in a variety of locations. Their bites can cause severe pain, skin infection and possible death in small children.

Always attempt to identify the cause of a bite or sting. This is useful in determining the correct treatment and will greatly reduce pain and suffering. Get medical treatment as soon as possible. The above guidelines indicate the type of situations you may face when in the bush.

The need for a well-trained first aider with an adequately stocked first aid kit when out in the bush cannot be over-emphasised.

Index

Page references in *italics* indicate illustrations.